AN ADVAITIC VIEW OF KANTIAN PHILOSOPHY

AN ADVAITIC VIEW OF KANTIAN PHILOSOPHY

Swami Shantidharmananda Saraswati

KALPAZ PUBLICATIONS
Delhi—110 052

AN ADVAITIC VIEW OF KANTIAN PHILOSOPHY
(Public Interest)

Rs. 540

ISBN: 81-7835-321-0

Published in 2005 in India by
Kalpaz Publications
C-30, Satyawati Nagar
Delhi-110 052
E-mail: kalpaz@hotmail.com

Laser Typesetting by: Varsha Graphics, Delhi
Printed at: Mehra Offset Printers, Delhi

Contents

	Preface	5
	Acknowledgements	9
	Introduction	17
1.	The Nature of True Philosophy	31
2.	The True Definition of a True Philosophy	37
3.	The Need of a Philosophy	55
4.	The Different Methods of Philosophy	61
5.	The Sanātana Method	75
6.	An Analysis of Self	81
7.	An Analysis of Perception	97
8.	The Universe and its Constitution	123
9.	How Sanatana view can correct Kant	141
10.	Conclusion	167
	Appendix I Kant and Shaivism—A Comparative Study	177
	Appendix II A Critical Analysis of Kant's Lecture on Enlightenment	180
	Appendix III Answers to Objections	198
	Index	203

Preface

Philosophy is a very vast, deep, tough and difficult subject as it is related to not only mans ethical, moral, social and cultural life but it also deals all aspects of the human life unto his Liberation. In this quest genius men all over the World have been working hard since the creation of the Universe. There is a very long consistent history in the East, particularly in India and in the West it is of a very short history. The basic difference in the East and West is that in the East the Sages were not under any sort of pressure whereas in the West almost all philosophers were not only under the direct influence of the socio-political situations, but also under the pressure of church and other religious institutions of their times. Thus it has been said that there is a radical difference between the Western and the Eastern methods of approach the pursuit of Philosophy. Western philosophers are generally distinguished from the Eastern by their exclusive focus on rational approach to the ultimate Reality of the Universe and Self, and in their paying not much attention or being totally indifferent to the methodology of super-sensuous intuition. Some historians of Western Philosophy have gone even to the extent of either rejecting or neglecting all Eastern thought as shot through with "faith" and not deserving of inclusion in such a chronicle. However, there were some exceptionally great mystics in the West too, who proclaimed the possibility of an intuitional approach to truth by transcending the realms of senses, understanding and reason. But most of them were the targets of suspicion and their supreme spiritual thoughts were doubted by church and other religious institutions due to their own superior attitude on the part of the logical and religious thinkers.

On a study of the history of Philosophy in the West we do come across variegated type of philosophers who have made diversified approaches to the problems of life and established several different schools of Philosophy which generally comprehend vast fields of observation, investigation and research, such as logic, epistemology, metaphysics, aesthetics, ethics, psychology and mysticism. In modern times however, the implications of the discoveries in physical science have practically become a part of the study of philosophy, for, they too claim to give total absolute happiness and it is to make life more easy, luxurious, comfortable and happy that physical science is exploiting the Nature. On the other hand, there are many in India, who think that an attempt to study and understand the methods and conclusions of the thinkers in the West is just misspent or draining or wastage of energy, holding, as they do, the view that the method of faith and intuition in philosophy mostly followed in India is the only practicable, meaningful, useful and trustworthy way. We need not take any one side of these extreme views of the traditional conservatives of either the West or the East. For, knowledge is neither Western nor Eastern, but it is Universal and Eternal.

It is also not true that the Indian philosophers abrogated reason as absolutely futile, though they emphasized its natural limits. There are certain schools of philosophy in India too which establish their systems exclusively on rational grounds without discrediting the value and need of intuition in any way. The Philosopher Adi Shankaracharya, who was an ardent adherent to Authority and revelation, made full to use of the powers of reason in founding his stupendous system and said that Vedanta (the Sanatana Method) is ornamented by the fact that its strength lies not merely in appealing to revelation only but along with reason and experience also. Adding, however, a note that reason unbridled which goes counter to revelation should be rejected as misleading.

In this present book I have used Science and Western Philosophy to show the inconsistencies in their method and conclusions of the difference branches of Science, Science as a whole and the different systems of philosophies of the West, thereby trying to gain mastery over the philosophy of Absolution (Vedanta). In this study it will be shown how the Vedanta is characterized by integrality in its meaning, method and scope, built on the foundations of the most systematic incisive logical analysis, and how it does not reject nothing as totally useless; though it accepts nothing without sifting it through the sieve of direct non-sensuous experience in super-sensuous inseams intuition. I expect this comparative study would certainly not only add something to the knowledge but also give deep insight to all those who wish to make a comparative study of the philosophies of some of the great Western thinkers and of the philosophy of the Vedanta (the Sanatana Eternal method), which is the culmination of Eastern thought.

The main aim of this study is to indicate and correct the inconsistencies of the greatest and earnest modernist Western philosopher Immanuel Kant, who has built up his critiques totally based on reasoning, even though he accepts intellectual antiques totally based on reasoning, even though he accepts intellectual intuition. Thus it is our duty to show the correct and right method of philosophy through a comparative study. It is true that it is not either feasible or possible to treat Kant's voluminous critiques line to line and word by word. Thus in the beginning I have tried to put the gist of his philosophy treating the main and major postulations of Kant based on which the rest of the book goes on. This study not only opens door but will prove to be a gateway for a dialogue between East and West in the field of further comparative study. This is just a suite beginning in the court of philosophy for the people to judge the difference between the Western paradigm and the Eastern wisdom. As stated before knowledge is not a personal property of anyone, but it is universal and eternal. This study will reveal that the Eastern wisdom, especially Vedanta, is the only true philosophy in each and every aspect by which one can attain Absolute Eternal Universal knowledge and experience one's own self as Absolute Existence-Consciousness-Bliss and attain liberation.

Acknowledgements

1

H.H. Shri Swami Shantidharmananda Saraswati has made a bold and original attempt to analyse the various features of the philosophy of Immanuel Kant from the standpoint of the philosophy of Sanatana Dharma (Vedanta). The work is a very serious attempt to demonstrate the charm and grandeur of Vedanta philosophy and its tenets in comparison with the thought system of perhaps the greatest western philosopher of the modern times Immanuel Kant.

The author has very successfully refuted the current argument among the so-called modernists, including many of the so-called free thinkers of the New Age', that the philosophical system of Sanatana dharma (Vedanta) is other-worldly and teaches man to run away from the world of realities he is living in, a lifeless dogma divorced from the facts of everyday life. This, in itself, is a great achievement. Vedanta teaches us that desires (Kama) and Money (artha) are not the supreme goals of the human life. If one leads this life without deviating from the path of Dharma (a religious and moral life), then he realizes, at a particular stage, that the supreme goal of life is Liberation (moksha). Even an intellectual understanding of this truth brings about what the author calls "a change in the vision of life." (p. 71)

Kantian philosophy is essentially confined within the limits of reason and sensory perception and therefore does not recognise a Supreme Reality which can be cognized only through non-sensuous intuitive experience. It should, however, be noted that this intuitive experience of Vedanta is entirely different from what Kant himself calls intuitions.

Kant's great achievement was that he recognizes that knowledge is not completely derived from sense-experience. In this respect, this system is much closer to Advaita Vedanta than that of either Locke or Hume.

It is heartening to note that the author gives due credit to Kant for making a thorough investigation of the powers of human reason. But he made the philosophically intellectual and philosophical culture and ethos that he inherited did not allow him to recognize that there was something beyond the reach of human reason and intellect. The author dwelling at length, upon the limitations of reason asserts that "the true nature of God and His creation cannot be intellectually grasped or comprehended, for logic is a proud child of dualist prejudice".

The author has successfully established the supremacy of Vedanta, especially Advaita Vedanta, giving a number of examples from the System of Kant, and by comparing them with the view of Sanatana Dharma.

Space, time, causation, things-in-themselves etc. are, according to Sanatana Dharma, illusory and phenomenal. The finite world of objects is characterized by name and form in time, space and causation. The Atman (the Self) is the only reality which cannot be characterized by name and form. Atman, the author asserts, is transcendental unity of consciousness which is responsible for our own feeling and experience of self-identity. It is the 'I', the one witness of all experiences. While Vedanta accepts the unity of consciousness, the supreme witness and unifier of all our experiences, as essentially non-dual, Absolute Knowledge, Absolute Existence and Absolute Bliss. Kant says they are dual and manifold.

By effectively asserting the logical and rational superiority of Vedanta as compared to western philosophical tradition, especially with the System of Kant, the author has made a remarkable contribution to comparative philosophy.

— • —

Swami Tattwamayananda
Sri Ramakrishna Ashrama, Vivekananda Vijnana Bhavanam,
P.O. Punkunnam, Thrissur, Kerala

— • —

2

I have gone through the monograph entitled 'Advaitic view of Kantian Philosophy' authored by Swami Shantidharmananda Saraswati. The following are chapter wise comments on the monograph.

In the introduction the author has presented a synopsis of the Kantian Philosophy. The synopsis is a faithful presentation of Kant's Philosophy.

In the first chapter Swamiji defines the true nature of philosophy. Philosophy, he argues, is not a study of thoughts of many schools; it is concerned with absolute consciousness, the knowledge of which leads man to inner peace and satisfaction. The philosophy of Sanatana Dharma is most suited to the purpose, argues Swamiji.

In the second chapter 'a true definition of true philosophy' has been formulated. Philosophy, in the author's view, is not just 'love for wisdom'; it is a moral and intellectual science which tries to explain the reality behind appearances by reducing the phenomena of the universe to the ultimate causes by the application of reason and law. Philosophy, it is further said, is the expression of the inner urge to know the Absolute and true philosophy is that which leads an aspirant to experience Absolute Knowledge as reality which is again consciousness and bliss, i.e., Non-dual Absolute. To achieve this Non-dual Absolute integral intuition is the only pathway. Distinctions between sense, understanding and reason have been pointed out and it has been also pointed out that intuition is not opposed to them; rather it embraces them all. In the same chapter classifications of philosophy into metaphysics, epistemology etc., have also been explained.

The third chapter underlines the need of philosophy to mankind. Man has rightful claim to reality and this claim can be fulfilled by philosophy alone.

The fourth chapter contains a statement of the different methods of philosophy. The fifth chapter explains the Sanatana or Vedantic method of philosophizing while the concept of Self in Sanatana Dharma has been elucidated in the sixth chapter. The exposition is alright. Prior to that various theories of Self in the western tradition have bene stated and their shortcomings have been pointed out.

An analysis of perception according to the Sanatana method is presented in seventh chapter with reference to the theories of Samkhya and Kant and also of Moore and William James etc.

The author examines the nature and constitution of universe in the eighth chapter. Phenomenal character of space and time and their transcendence in the Supreme Self according to the Sanatana doctrine have been clearly explained. He also analyses the concept of causality with reference to the views of James Jeans and Eddington and finally concludes that the Sanatana view which believes that the effect is not really different from the cause is the most plausible view.

The ninth chapter-how Sanatana view can correct Kant-is the main theme of the present book.

The author rightly gives credit to kant for conceiving the possibility of 'intellectual intuition' and for investigating the powers and limits of reason (p. 139). However if Kant could not visualize the impossibility of 'intellectual intuition' becoming a reality of experience, the fault is not his individual fault. He has no backing of a tradition where non-sensuous intuition is accepted as a valid mode of experience.

The concluding chapter is a sort of resume of the views of Kant and its inadequacy. It is suggested that a corrective to Kant's agnosticism is available in the Sanatana philosophy.

Appendix 1 and 2, viz., Saivism vs Kant and Enlightenment add to the value of the book.

S. Mishra
Head, Deptt. of Philosophy,
DDU Gorakhpur University, Gorakhpur

— • —

3

The book entitled 'An Advaitic view of Kantian Philosophy' has been written by Swami Ji with an honest intellectual rather than spiritual commitments.

Definitely the book has contributed in to my individual understanding of complicated philosophical ideas, arguments and thinking and contradictions and inconsistencies in many respects.

Kant has been a philosopher inviting intellectual exercises for not only linguistic tough comprehensibility but also for the vast, rich and complicated philosophical theories and their implications involved therewith. The studies on Kant have accepted and elaborated how Kant had made an attempt to evaluate, scrutinize and extracted the positive aspects to construct a positive Epistemology, Ontology and Moral philosophy in his philosophical thinking. By extracting all the essential and acceptable ideas from his preceding philosophers he did make an attempt to provide theory of knowledge that he claimed to be universal, objective, certain and necessary having the qualities of both the rationalist and empiricists. For this purpose he claimed to have criticized both for their inconsistencies. In the process he separated the knowledge from faith and rather claimed to limit the domain of knowledge for making the room for faith. This was essential for his commitment towards moral philosophies. All these objectives put together and Kant's own linguistic distinction might have been the reason for such a classical expression to communicate his philosophical arguments in his three Critiques and other writings. Attempting upon such a greater Moral, Epistemological and Ontological objectives Kant did provide an exhaustive analyses that have virtues as well as limitations.

The author's attempt to point out the persistent inconsistencies of Kantian philosophical thinking and make it consistent by viewing and supplementing the Sanatana philosophical arguments and theories for providing contributory direction above than merely done in a comparative study by drawing lines between similarities and differences.

This particular attempt with reference to Unity of Apperception and Pure Self, and the difference drawn between Immaturity (Kant) and Ignorance (Sanatana) will prove interesting and thought provoking to all readers. Thus the book must be published for its anticipated contribution and original flavour.

With my limited understanding, I am giving my observations as follows:

The book will provide an innovative insight for the students of philosophy for its technical argumentation and for general readers interested in fundamental philosophical queries as it has dealt with the meaning, nature, need and methods of philosophical studies in popular and technical sense. His attempt to deal with the question, how Science fails to provide a thorough and philosophical insights in the Mathematics, Physics, Chemistry, Biology, Psychology, Sociology and Ethics as Science of Human behaviour has been an interesting reading.

A comparison between Eastern and Western approaches and methods is objective while considering Eastern approach as not the blind faith but the method of faith and intuition as only practical, useful and trustworthy and Western methods stick to rational elaboration of important philosophical issues. His objective attempts have been reflected in the following words, 'As knowledge is neither Western nor Eastern, but universal. It is not true that the Eastern Philosopher abrogated reason as futile, though they emphasized its natural limits. There are certain Philosophical schools in the East too, which establish their systems exclusively on the rational grounds without discrediting the value and need of intuition in any way'.

The book reflects the author's vast reading with rich contents of Eastern approach from early Vedas to Vedanta under one heading Sanatana and Western approach from early Greek to contemporary philosophies of Bertrand Russell and James Jeans.

The chapters dealing with Self, Perception and the Universe and its constitution provide an exhaustive elaboration of the arguments as required for the purpose that is to show the inconsistencies of Kant's philosophy and providing the Supremacy of the Sanatana deliberations and arguments. This seems to be the prime objective of the under publishing manuscript.

The chapter *'How Sanatan View Can Correct Kant'* shows the writer's skill to cut through the problems on the question of knowledge of things in themselves and attempt to resolve it by providing the Sanatan philosophy of the Absolute Reality. His attempts to extend the horizon of Intuition in the specific sense with particular objective might be proved very interesting for many readers and is very much conducive to Indian Philosophy. The same opinion may apply to the thought on Moral principles as well.

The appendix I & II motivates to go for further readings on the subjects. The comparison between three parts of dialects i.e. thesis, antithesis and synthesis and three powers of Shiva and Shakti i.e. creation, development and destruction provides an interesting reading but leaves the understanding of the knot how the exclusively epistemological problem can be solved by highly metaphysical deliberations.

Keeping all the above points in mind, this manuscript must be published for the sake of intellectual distinction and to begin a debate between the East and the West.

Dr. Indoo (Pandey) Khaduri
Reader, Deptt. of Philosophy, HNB Garhwal University
Srinagar, Pauri Garhwal, Uttaranchal

— • —

4

It was revealing to go through the critique written by the Swamiji. What a stupendous task he has taken up and completed successfully. However, I have gone through his book line by line out of my respect for the venerable personality of the Swamy on the one hand and because it is a comparative study of the prominent currents of thoughts from the west and the east on the other hand. I was able to grasp many of the details the author has so beautifully worked out to make Kantian Philosophy understandable to the uninitiated.

The Advaitic view that the world is unreal is stressed time and again. But the aim of philosophy, the meaning of philosophy, the difference between eastern and western approaches to philosophy as a means to realize the essence of life and such other vital points are well worked.

Further dealing with perception, it has been elaborately detailed that the consciousness is three fold as cognizing, cognitive and object. This identification is possible because the essential consciousness that underlies the cognizing, cognitive and objects as their reality is one and the same universal consciousness. (p. 103).

The analysis of the western systems is bold and free. We students of Indian philosophy need to know the western systems to confidently justify the real worth and value of what we know.

Swamiji has opened a new chapter in the area of understanding and appreciating new line of thinking available outside India.

The comparative study is highly informative and extremely useful in pinpointing the loopholes and strong points. Studies of this type are most welcome as they are highly beneficial.

Dr. S.R. Leela
Professor & Head, Department of Sanskrit
UMKRV College for Women
Jayanaga, Bangalore

— • —

5

I had great pleasure in reading the manuscript of "An Advaitic view of Kantian Philosophy" by Swami Shantidharmananda Saraswati. The following are my comments. Swamiji's work under the above title is a bold attempt in understanding Kant's Philosophy from the point of view of Vedanta, the Sanatana philosophy of India. He has done a great job in presenting Kant's philosophy for the first time in the context of Indian Philosophy. Swamiji's understanding of Kant is very deep. His mastery of Vedanta is equally profound. He has shown that Kant's philosophy fails short of reaching the height of metaphysics of Vedanta. Kant has not overcome the limitations of reason which he has accepted as final. But Vedanta goes beyond Reason to reach the Absolute, the Brahman.

Swamiji's work when published will create new interest in understanding the west in terms of our Indian Philosophy. Indian philosophy has been neglected too long by the Indians, so this kind of new venture is most welcome. Hope all will benefit by this work.

Prof. R.C. Pradhan,
Dept. of Philosophy, University of Hyderabad,
Gochibowli, Hyderabad, A.P. 500046, India

— • —

Introduction

A Synopsis of Kantian Philosophy

In my view what Kantian Philosophy says as I have understood can be put briefly as follows:

Whatever Kant has said is within the realms of reason and perception, which have their own limitations. Thus the whole of Kantian Philosophy is limited to the materialistic world. Because in his philosophy, sometimes called Critical Philosophy which is contained in his *Critique of Pure Reason* (1781), he has examined the basic principles of human knowledge and created a general epistemology. Like earlier philosophers, Kant differentiated modes of thinking into analytic and synthetic propositions. An analytic proposition is one in which the predicate is contained in the subject, as in the statement—"Black Houses are Houses." The truth of this type of proposition is evident, because to state the opposite would be to make the proposition self-contradictory. Such propositions are called analytical because truth is discovered by analysis of the concept itself. Synthetic propositions, on the other hand, are those that cannot be arrived at by pure analysis, as in the statement—"The house is black." All the common propositions that result from experience of the world are synthetic propositions. They according to Kant, can also be divided into two other types: empirical and *a priori*. Empirical propositions depend entirely on sense perception, but *a priori* propositions have a fundamental validity and are not based on such perception. The difference between these two types of proposition may be illustrated by the empirical. "The house is black" and the *a priori* "Two plus two makes four." Kant's thesis in the *critique* is that it is possible to make synthetic *a priori* judgements. This philosophical position is usually known as transcendentalism. In describing how this type of judgement is possible, Kant regarded the objects of the material world as fundamentally unknowable; from the point of view of reason, they serve merely as the raw material from which sensations are formed. Objects of themselves have no existence, and space and time exist only as part of the mind, as 'intuitions' by which perceptions are measured and judged.

In addition to these intuitions, Kant stated that a number of *a priori* concepts which he called categories, also exist. He divided the categories into four groups—those concerning *quantity,* which are unity, plurality and totality; those concerning *quality,* which are reality, negation and limitation; those concerning *relation,* which are substance and accident, cause-and-effect, and reciprocity; and those concerning *modality,* which are possibility, existence and necessity. The intuitions and the categories can be applied to make judgements about experiences and perceptions, but cannot, according to Kant, be applied to abstract ideas such as freedom and existence without leading to inconsistencies in the form of pairs of contradictory propositions or *antinomies,* in which both members of each pair can be proved true.

Kant's ethical ideas are a logical outcome of his belief in the fundamental freedom of the individual as stated in his *Critique of Practical Reason* (1788). This freedom he did not regard as the lawless freedom of anarchy, but rather as the freedom of self-government, the freedom to obey consciously the laws of the universe as revealed by reason. He believed that the welfare of each individual should properly be regarded as an end in itself and that the world was progressing toward an ideal society in which reason would bind every law giver to make his laws in such a way that they could have sprung from the united will of entire people, and to regard every subject, in so far as he wishes to be a citizen, on the basis of whether he has conformed to that will.

In the *Metaphysics of Ethics* (1797) Kant described his ethical system, which is based on a belief that the reason is the final authority for Morality. Actions of any sort, he believed, must bo undertaken from a sense of duty dictated by reason, and no action performed for expediency or solely in obedience to law or custom can be regarded as moral. Kant described two types of commands given by reason: the *hypothetical imperative,* which dictates a given course of action to reach a specific end; and the *categorical imperative,* which dictates a course of action that must be followed because of its rightness and necessity. The categorical imperative is the basis of morality and was stated by Kant in these words: "Act as if the maxim of thy (your) action were to become through your will a general natural law."

In other words we can put Kantian Philosophy in a descriptive manner as follows: Before Kant, there were two main trends of thought in the transition period of Modern Philosophy, namely—Rationalism and Empiricism. The thinkers of the Renaissance period had combined both in their writings. But later on the two tendencies got separated and the result was the rationalistic thought of Descartes, Spinoza and Leibnitz, on one hand, and the empirical thought of Locke, Berkeley and Hume on the other. Both sides were one sided, and so dogmatic, and a need was felt for a fresh reconstruction of thought and this was undertaken eminently by Kant.

Kant's Relation to Previous Thoughts

Kant agreed with the Rationalists by admitting universal and necessary truths, but rejected their doctrine of innate ideas as the source of truths. He argued with the Empiricists by upholding experience to be the source of all knowledge, but rejected their sensationalism. So he critically examined the positions of both Rationalism and Empiricism which resulted in a fresh reconstruction of thought by accepting elementary truths in them and rejecting their dogmatic extremes. The principal works in which Kant presents his epoch-making philosophical thoughts are—Critique of Pure Reason, Critique of Principal (Practical) Reason and Critique of Judgement.

Kant's New Interpretation of Experience

According to Kant the world of Experience does not consist of mere disconnected *impressions* (sensations) passively received but is a connected system of phenomena, which is made as such by the activity of our mind out of the sensations passively received. Thus the sensations are the raw material of our knowledge. But the forms or relations in which the world of objects appears to our experience are the contributions of the mind (the moulds in which the material is shaped by our understanding). Therefore the objective world of experience is a construction of our mind. This is *idealistic,* for the world of experience being made dependent upon constructive activity of mind. But this idealism is not subjective. The world of phenomena, though dependent on the mind for being what it is, does not depend entirely on the passive experience of individual minds. On the contrary, it is a construction of the common mind of humanity; so it appears to be objective to and independent of individual minds. This position of Kant developed logically later into the objective idealism of Fichte and Hegel. The difference between the Kantian position and that of other later idealists lies in this that the world of experience was not made by Kant entirely dependent on mind as shown above, for the matter (thing-in-itself, as called by Kant) of it, he held, comes to it from an outer source as our feelings (sensations)—only the forms being contributed by the mind, while the later Idealistic thinkers made both the matter and the form as furnished by the mind. Here his followers were more consistent than Kant himself.

Kant's Epistemology

Kant begins with an examination of the nature, source and extent of human knowledge. Kant finds two factors in experience by critical analysis—a matter and a form. Sensations are the raw materials of knowledge received from without, which are arranged under certain forms contributed to them by the mind. Our knowledge of individual objects and their relations, which make up our actual world of experience, is the product of both factors. Experience as we have it is not mere matter (sensations) nor mere form (conception). "Conception without perception is empty, perception with conception is blind"—according to Kant. The question now is how do they both build up experience. The answer to this question is given in his famous work Critique of Pure Reason, in which he presents his theory of knowledge, forming the basis and the most important part, of his philosophical thought. It is as follows:

(a) Nature of Knowledge: He calls all knowledge as collections of Judgements. They are of two kinds—*a posteriori* and *a priori*. By the former he means such knowledge or judgements which come from experience; by the latter he means judgements which are not derived from experience, but follow from the very nature of thought. Further he divides *a priori* judgements into two—analytic and synthetic. Analytic judgements are those which are derived from the idea or thought of an object, for example, a triangle is a figure, in this experience the predicate figure does not give any knowledge about a triangle, but only states explicitly what is already contained implicitly in the idea of a triangle. Such judgements are of course, *necessary,* as they follow from the very concept about which predication is made. Hence they are *a priori,* i.e., they do not require any reference to actual experience of an object for the prediction. Synthetic *a priori* judgements are found in mathematics and sciences. For example: A triangle has its three angles equal to 180° or that every event must have a cause for its occurence. Such judgements are by their very nature universal and necessarily true for all triangles and all events, and accepted as undeniable by all minds. Thus they are *a priori.* For they cannot be derived from actual experience which has to do with particular triangles or events. They are again not even got by generalisation from experience. Because no generalisation from experience of individual objects or of particular events can give us universal and necessary truths. Generalisation cannot go beyond what has been actually experienced. It can give us knowledge of what has been hitherto, but never of what must be for all times and places. Hence such judgements cannot be *a posteriori,* but must be *a priori.* And as they are not analytic, they must be synthetic, because they extend our knowledge beyond actual experience.

(b) Origin of knowledge: If our mathematical and scientific truths are *a priori,* then, how were they formed? For this, when one analyses the nature of objects and their relations as furnished by experience finds in them two factors—a matter and a form. The matter is the particular variable element in them; as for instance; the sensations in our experience of a particular object. The form is the universal and permanent factor. The form which is the universal and permanent factor is the character in them, for example, the way in which we experience the sensations, as outside of each other, or as following each other, or as combined into a unity, or as occuring in a fixed order. These are some of the permanent and universal forms in which we have our sensible experience. Now the matter of an experience is received passively: it comes to us independently of any activity of our mind from that which Kant calls "things-in-themselves". But the forms do not come so. They are the ways in which the mind by its very nature arranges the matter of experience—they are the moulds, as it were, into which the sensations are cast. The result is that our experience of even a sensible object is never pure matter (i.e., sensations) nor pure form (i.e., conceptions), but the product of both factors. The matter becomes a changeable factor as it comes independently from the mind, whereas the form is not so, as it is contributed by the mind by its very nature. And as all minds have a common nature, the forms in which the world of experience appears to us is common for all minds. Hence the objectivity and independence ascribed to nature. Hence also the universality ascribed to the relations of objects and to the laws of events in nature. The forms are but relations under which the common mind of humanity arranges its experience or fashions it.

This is the general position of Kant regarding theory of knowledge. Now let us see how Kant builds upon experience under this position. For that Kant recognises three levels of experience—that of sense, of understanding and of reason. The first accounts for intuition of senses, the second deals the ordering of these intuitions into objects and thus a relation. These two levels fall within the sphere of our phenomenal experience. The third goes beyond it, having to do with certain ideas or ideals, which though operative in our experience, have really no place in the world of experience. They never appear as objects of knowledge, hence they are noumenal and are matters of faith only. Thus—

(a) *Intuitions of Sense:* Sensations as they appear in our experience are perceived either as outside of each other or as successive, i.e., they come to our mind as already arranged in the relations of space and time. These relations are the forms supplied by the mind at its lowest sense level of experience. Space and Time are therefore the forms of intuitions of sense—called by Kant as *pure intuitions.* Because these forms are universal and necessary and are at the basis of all mathematical and scientific truths.

(b) *The Categories:* The intuitions of sense are the materials on which understanding works according to the forms applied by itself. These forms are called by Kant as *categories.* They are rather concepts or relations under which the sensible objects already arranged in space and time are brought further for the building of the world of phenomena as we experience it. These categories are classified by Kant under four heads and he recognises three forms under each correlating with judgement as follows:

Categories	*Judgements*
(i) Quantity	
(a) Unity	universal
(b) Plurality	particular
(c) Totality	singular
(ii) Quality	
(a) Reality	affirmative
(b) Negation	negative
(c) Limitation	infinite
(iii) Relation	
(a) Inherence and subsistence	categorical
(b) Causality and dependence	hypothetical
(c) Community	disjunctive
(iv) Modality	
(a) Possibility-impossibility	problematic
(b) Existence-non existence	assertoric
(c) Necessity-contingence	apodictic.

This table shows clearly that Kant derived them from the logical classification of propositions. But the forms under each class are his own way of regarding them. Two of them are important as emphasising two aspects of the world of experience; namely—categories of substance and causality, which are the subjects of physical science. These categories are the *a priori* forms of the understanding, while space and time are the *a priori* forms of perception. The understanding works according to its universal and necessary forms, and thus prescribes its own laws to them. Nature, as we know it, is thus not independent of mind—but constructed according to its inherent modes of thought out of materials furnished by sense-experience. Hence it is possible to enlarge our view about nature by imagining (i.e. with the help of reasoning) what is beyond actual sensual experience. For, if nature is a creation of mind, the mind in thinking of the *possible* must by its very nature think it in the forms in which it has made the *actual*. Hence follow the universality and necessity of the laws of nature. They are so, not because they belong to nature independently of mind, but because they are the universal and necessary constructions of mind. The Self which constructs such nature is not, however, the individual Empirical Self which is distinct for each person and has many limitations, but the Universal Self of all human beings, which transcends the empirical level of mind. As this is one for all human beings, for, the experiences of all are of a common nature. There is a unity of minds here, Kant calls this as the Transcendental Unity of Appreception (transcedent, because it is not an object of experience but makes all experience possible), which is the source of all the categories under which the world of nature is apprehended by us.

The world of experience as constructed by the mind is the phenomenal world. So the categories or forms under which we experience it have application to this world of phenomena only. They have no application beyond it. Anything beyond it, i.e., the world of noumena (which is also recognised by Kant) must remain therefore unknown and unknowable. They can never be objects of knowledge, but of faith only. But is there any such noumenal world? To answer this he developed the next higher level of experience which Kant called as—the Ideas of Reason.

(c) *Ideas of Reason:* There is a demand in the human mind to seek unity of experience. This demand has its source in the very unity of consciousness. Out of this unity (the unity of apperception—as called by Kant) arise all synthetic activities of the mind. It is the source of the synthetic activity of mind under the forms of space and time at the perceptual level. It is also the source of categories under which the materials of perception are synthesised at the level of understanding. So, at the levels of intuition and understanding, however, the human mind deals with the phenomenal side of experience, which is limited and conditioned by its very nature. Our experience at these levels can never go beyond the phenomena as thus limited and conditioned. The forms of perception and of understanding have, therefore, operation within this limited and conditioned world of phenomena. But the human mind, in its demand for unity of experience, can never be satisfied with the limited and the conditioned. Hence it seeks to go beyond the phenomenal level to the unlimited and the unconditioned to complete its work of unification. In doing so, it uses certain ideal forms which have been called by Kant as—Ideas of Reasons. They are, in their very nature, pure concepts which can never be constituted as objects of knowledge nor have their operation within the phenomenal world. Hence they are not constituitive of this experience, as the forms of perception and understanding are. But they have a value of their own even for our phenomenal experience, as the ideals towards which this experience must proceed in its search for unity. They are, therefore, called as regulative principles by Kant. Kant recognises three such ideas, namely:

1. The idea of the soul as a simple substance at the back of the activities of the mind;
2. The idea of the world as a totality, or a whole unlimited or infinite;
3. The idea of an unconditioned first cause of the world of matter and mind, i.e., God.

The first idea gives rise to speculative psychology; the second to, speculative cosmology; and the third to speculative theology. Any attempt to make these ideas objects of knowledge by trying to bring them under the categories of understanding will land us in fictions and contradictions, from which we cannot free ourselves at this level. These fictions under the first head he calls—1. Paralogisms of Reason; and the contradictions in the second and third heads as; 2. Antinomies of Reason. They can be put as follows: (a) *Paralogisms of Speculative or Rational Psychology*—The unity of consciousness has led the rationalists to suppose that there is a simple, self-existent, indecomposible, self-identical Soul substance. The Empiricists on the other hand, prove that we have no such knowledge of a soul as a substance that remains identically the same in our experience of Self. We cannot therefore prove, theoretically, the existence of free will and immortality of the Soul using the usual modes of reasoning. The conclusion does not follow from the premises. Hence the paralogisms. (b) *Antinomies of speculative cosmology:* In the attempt to prove the existence of a universe as a totality, unconditioned and infinite, and of freedom and God, we are landed in inevitable antinomies or contradictions in which a thesis and an antithesis are both possible to prove by reasoning. There are four such antinomies: Thus:

(i) The antinomy of creation. *Thesis*—The world must have a beginning in time and be enclosed in finite space. *Antithesis*—The world is eternal and infinite.

(ii) The antinomy of simple. *Thesis*—The world is ultimately divisible into simple parts which cannot be further divided. *Antithesis*—The world is a compound of parts subject to no further division, and thus no simple thing exists in the world.

(iii) The antinomy of freedom. *Thesis*—There is freedom, there are phenomenal events that cannot be accounted for by necessity. *Antithesis*—There is no freedom, but everything takes place entirely according to necessary laws of nature.

(iv) The antinomy of theology: *Thesis*—There is a necessary being either as part or as a cause of the world. *Antithesis*—There exists neither within nor without the world an absolutely necessary Being.

About these antinomies Kant holds that when the universe is treated as an object of knowledge, contradictory propositions can be maintained, because the propositions can be proved and disproved. But of the four antinomies, Kant holds that the first two are both false; the last two can be true, if they refer to different worlds. If the ideas are applied to the world of phenomena, they involve the contradictions; but not, if they are applied to the world of noumena. The ideas of free will and unconditional being are possible as noumenal objects; while the ideas of necessity and conditioned being are true as objects of the phenomenal world. The possibility of the former alternative brings in Kant's ethical theory, from the standpoint of which the ideas of free will and God are held to be valid as postulates.

Kant's Ethical Theory

Kant's ethical theory, like his theory of knowledge is also unique in the history of modern western philosophy. He presents his theory of morality in two books: *"Metaphysics of Morality"* and *"Critique of Pure Practical Reason"*. In these he has established a view about human nature, which does not places man above the empirical or the phenomenal level, but places in a noumenal or intelligible level as called by Kant himself.

The essence of man is his reason. This reason has a theoretical and a practical side. It is a faculty of knowledge, and a faculty of will, both. In the former aspect it builds up the world of experience, while in the latter aspect it gives us world of morality. In both the aspects it is the source of *a priori* forms-- which are embodied in universal and necessary truths. Just as in the sphere of knowledge we find universal and necessary laws, similarly we recognise universal and necessary laws in the sphere of practice. The difference between them is that in the former they relate to things 'as they are', in the latter they relate to actions 'as they ought to be'. Man has a double nature, as an empirical being—subject to the necessary laws of phenomena and as an intelligible being—free from them, but subject to laws of practical reason. But, as these laws are the laws of his own will which is his innermost essence, man is autonomous here, i.e., he lays down laws to himself and obeys them freely. One such fundamental law is the principle of morality, which Kant formulates as "Act so that the maxim of thy action may serve as a universal rule". But the law stated thus is too abstract and formal, hence, he gives a more concrete and practical statement to the law in another form—"So act as to treat humanity, whether in this own person or in that of any other, in every case as an end and never as a means only." This principle of morality, stated in either form, Kant calls it as *categoral imperative.* As such it is the ultimate base of all other moral laws which are generally accepted as binding on man. He distinguishes this principle from which he calls as *Hypothetical Imperative,* which can never be universally valid and binding. The former is unconditional as following from the very nature of reason as pure will which is independent of all inclinations or impulses; the latter relates to actions determined by instincts and impulses. By this Kant holds that "nothing can possibly be conceived, in this world or even out of it, which can be called to be good without qualification, except a good will". For a will that is determined by inclinations or desires or feelings can never be universal, they being different for different persons. Nor can a 'will' be determined by the consideration of consequences as motives can be categorised or absolute. Such will can only be hypothetical or relative, depending upon the consequence desired. On the other hand, a will that is determined out of reference for the law of reason—which is its own law, can truly be a good will. The law again depending on no other considerations but its own worth, is unconditionally binding. Hence it is called as the categorical imperative.

Thus Kant puts the moral law above the empirical level of life which is conditioned in its very nature. In doing so, he introduces a dualism here between the moral ideal and the ordinary life of man which has to be lived morally. The gap between the two appears to be absolute here. The ideal is too rigorous. How far the principle of morality as formulated by him is practically possible is a question.

On the basis of this high conception of morality Kant goes on, next, to indicate certain ideas which are involved in or deducible from it. These ideas he calls "Postulates of Morality. He recognises them in three divisions:

(1) The postulate of freedom,
(2) The postulate of the immortality of Soul, and
(3) The postulate of the existence of God.

The subject of these three postulates have been treated as Ideas of Reason in his critique of Pure Reason. They have been shown there to be matters of faith and not objects of knowledge. Here Kant goes on to justify the faith, as implicated in the very nature of the moral life as it ought to be lived according to him. Thus:

(a) *The Postulate of Freedom:* The categorical imperative comes to our consciousness as an ought demanding absolute obedience of the self. But an *ought* implies a *can*. There can be no law binding for us unless we have the capacity to obey it. This capacity implies a freedom of the will. Thus the freedom has to be there in the very possibility of moral life. In this sense freedom is a postulate of morality.

(b) *The Postulate of Immortality:* Man has a double nature the empirical and the intelligible. His intelligible self, which is his true nature demands an absolute obedience to the moral law: the law of duty. The empirical self, again, demands happiness as the recompense for the virtuous life lived according to the law of duty. But in the actual conditions of human life as lived in this world, happiness in not found to go invariably with a virtuous life. Hence the demand for recompense needs that, it will come in a future life, which implies that the Self must be immortal. Hence immortality is also a postulate of the moral life.

(c) *Postulates of the Existence of God:* The demand of recompose of virtue with happiness in a future life requires that there must be an eternal person of infinite wisdom and goodness and of unlimited power for the dispensation of the reward or punishment for the good or bad life lived by man. And this implies the existence of a dispenser. This is the postulate of the existence of God involved in the moral life.

The Critique of Judgement

There are several dualisms involved in the thoughts of Kant as presented in his critique of Pure and Practical Reasons. Kant has attempted to reconcile these dualisms in his book *"Critique of Pure Judgement"*, through the Aesthetic and Teleological aspects of Nature and of Human life. Thus this third book may be said to complete his system.

This a brief description of Kantian thoughts. Now in this book we will be critically analysing and be going through a microscopic examination trying to detect the philosophical mistakes, mispostulates, faults, errors, etc. and try to correct him through the Sanatana (Vedanta) philosophical method. His treatment regarding the different aspects of philosophy is totally wrong. It seems that the western thinkers surely had a wrong perception of the purpose, scope and aspects of Philosophy. Therefore we will be discussing in detail the basic need and purpose, scope as well as aspects of philosophy according to the Sanatana method, i.e., the eternal human method, the non-dual method. We will try to rectify and show that the Sanatana perspective is the only perfect and complete philosophy in all aspects.

I expect that the readers will be able to grasp the reality lying behind Kant's tricky reasoning, inferences, implications and imaginations, which are surely leading people into a lot of confusion and miseries. I wish the readers to realise the truth lying behind the postulations of the Sanatana method and experience themselves as pure-absolute existence-consciousness-bliss; at the same time lead an active life of joy in this illusory world without any miseries. I wish all a successful spiritual life.

Hari Om Tatsat.

1

The Nature of True Philosophy

It is true that a proper approach to the subject of the higher analysis of life in the language of the modern mind is long overdue. Even though a response to this need has been attempted by some scholars, the result in most cases was such that it evoked either the intellectual or emotional or materialistic side independently and man was not touched in his true sense—the Being. One has to deal human nature in its completeness and not merely a side of it. Mathematics, Physics, Chemistry, Biology, Psychology, Metaphysics, Mysticism, etc... developed a tendency to specialisation and became almost reserved to one branch only. This was not a desirable state of affair, because it encouraged a false unliked division in what in fact is an indivisible unity. We cannot just amputate a limb of a living body and then succeed in taking a decision about the true nature of the whole organism, because the study of life is many sided and very complicated. A conclusive rational knowledge of it involves a study of many minute things upto their ultimate causes beyond empirical observation. Therefore, the purely logical method of Philosophy or the way of feeling which different schools advocate cannot independently satisfy human aspiration. Because human aspiration always rises as a whole by all means. Therefore, to follow a systematic thinking upto its final limits would force one to give due attention to the laws of all different aspects of life. The seeker of truth has a difficult task to perform, as he cannot affiliate himself to any particular branch of learning and at the same time he cannot even ignore the many manifold character of knowledge and its means.

It is true that a scientific spirit is necessary in any study of philosophy but still science cannot satisfy the vital urges in Man. The main and major problem begins with the study of man himself and in searching the True Man, i.e., Soul (Atman); which is the highest principle of existence. While considering man as an individual, the problem of perception or knowledge of the external world will be a natural corollary. Right perception is a correct comprehension of fact. Therefore a thorough study of the composition of the universe which presents itself by different means before perception becomes the subject of critical analysis. It is to be decided whether the universe is real in the same sense as it appears, or it has some other meaning. Similarly a recognition of the inadequacy of all empirical experiences in its various forms forces the intellect to study the true nature of the Absolute, the True Man, i.e., Soul (Atman).

The purpose of Philosophy has been said as to trace the presence of the organic movement or process of reason in nature, in human mind, in all social institutions, in the history of nations and in the progressive advancement of the world. This means that Philosophy is the rationality behind science, psychology, sociology, ethics, politics, law and world history, in addition to its function of determining the significance of art and religion. Therefore a comprehensive complete Philosophy should be able to explain the ultimate rationale of all branches of knowledge governing all the different fields of life. For this, one has to understand the true nature of absolute truth. Because truth cannot be encountered in any one form alone, for it has atleast three degrees of manifestation. The Absolute, The Empirical and The Apparent. All the various questions that arise in Philosophy will have to be answered from these three different levels of Judgement.

How Science Fails as a Philosophy

A Philosophy in its true sense has to be naturally inseparable from universality of vision. Therefore it has to start from the study of the most basic fact of human perception, i.e., Nature, in all its externality and extremities.

Mathematics. The extreme content of the extroverted consciousness is the astronomical universe with its mathematical laws. In the cosmos physical bodies hang loosely with apparently no connection with each other, except for some gravitational pull and influence of an unknown power which is keeping them at a distance. It is true that mathematics is not identified to astronomy but they are very closely interrelated.

Due to this interrelation it is said that mathematical laws are also under the influence of the unknown power. Science does not say anything about that unknown power.

Physics. Even though physics tries to go deeper into the structure and content of this diversified external universe and discovers electoro-magnetic fields and other forces determining the nature, function and relationship of the physical bodies, but still Physics does not know about that underlying universal continuum into which all these physical bodies, finally fuse and coalesce.

Chemistry. On the other hand, Chemistry deals with the reactions that substances set up in their combinations as elements capable of a mutual relationship within their physical limits.

Thus a total true Human Philosophy is not explained either by Physics, Chemistry and Mathematics or by any other branch of Science. Because living beings are not mere physical bodies or substances intimately related. Therefore the life principle cannot be easily defined, thereby eludes all possibilities of determination in physical terms. Because the principles governing the inorganic things cannot be applied on organic things. Growth, evolution and above all a kind of self competency which exists and asserts in every living body are specialities in themselves.

Biology. Even Biology fails to determine the nature of absolute which is the underlying universal substratum of all human and non-human living organisms. Because Biology binds itself to the study of life only pointing out a thinking faculty in certain living being.

Psychology. Psychology, another branch of science, tries to deal with that Thinking element. The Behaviourist Gestalt, Hormic and all other theories of the psyche are only attempts to understand the peculiar expression of consciousness which divides itself into many forms familiarly known as thought, feeling, emotion, violition, memory, discrimination, self-affirmation, etc... Even though this branch of Science-Psychology, which classifies different faculties of human psyche, has differentiated man from animal; but still it is inconsistent, as it does not deal with mutual human relationship.

Sociology. For that one has to study Sociology. This deals with the Human relationships and their requirements within a society forming an important branch of investigation. This involves the details of anthropology too, which will lead to the more complex relations of political institutions, NGO's, charitable institutions, etc. necessitated by the circumstances of the group living and also the interests of the communities into which people form themselves. Sociology cannot determine and finalise any proper social system too because it depends again on human conduct.

Ethics. Ethics tries to give a final form to human conduct. Human conduct has to be and is actually regulated by mutual consent, external pressure or a moral sense predominant in some. At this stage an unending conflict begins between the ethical and political rules of groups of mankind which crystallize the laws of countries or nations leading to competition, exploitation and chaos in the universe. Therefore the legal codes have to consider the implications depending on the march of world history which exhibits a logical hand in all its indeterminable movements, hinting at the operation of the universal laws transcending humanity and yet immanent in it at all times. It is here that ethics and sociology also fail. Similarly the reader has to imply about all other branches of science.

Necessity of Philosophy

It is with this preamble that Philosophy has to commence the working out of its purpose. It has become an inherent habit of Human-Enterprises not to generally extend and evolve themselves to the universal. They have always parochial objectives and narrow mindedness due to which even Philosophy has been forced to narrow itself to the confined limits of human-psychological urges and social exigencies. There have been 'Philosophies' of subjects or approaches rather than a true philosophy wide enough to embrace the living principles animating all branches of human knowledge.

Humanity's longing has been not for learning the branches or the constitution of social institution, but the longing is for an absolute total inner peace with a satisfaction that the goal has been reached. The wanderings of the mind in the fields of external research have not brought the desired result, and man is today worse than an animal without any political and/or ethical value. The reason is an obvious misapprehension of what is good and an application of the wrong means in an attempt to reach the good. Therefore a mere study of Philosopical thoughts of the great thinkers in the manner of a history (this will be shown in chapter 4) will not suffice. Because Philosophy in its core is not simply the teachings of the many schools, but a vital content of absolute consciousness in its generality.

East and West

It has been said that there is a radical difference between the western and the eastern methods of approach in the pursuit of Philosophy. Western Philosophers are generally distinguished from the Eastern by the exclusively rational approach to the ultimate reality of the Universe and in their paying not much attention to or being totally indifferent to the method of intuition. Some historians of the Western Philosophy have gone even to the extent of dubbing all Eastern thought as outcome of "Blind faith" thus does not deserve inclusion in such a chronicle (History of Philosophy). No doubt, there were some exceptionally great mystics in the west too, who proclaimed the possibility of an intuitional approach to truth by transcending the realms of sense, understanding and reason. But they were mostly the targets of suspicion due to superior attitude on the part of the logical thinkers. After studying the history of Philosophy in the West we come across variegated types of Philosophers who make diverse approaches to the problems of life and established several schools of philosophy which generally comprehend inconsistently vast fields of observation, investigation and research. Such as logic, epistemology, metaphysics, ethics, aesthetics, pyschology and mysticism. As it is in the West about the East, similarly it is in the East about the West. There are many in the East who think that an attempt to study and understand the methods and conclusion of the Western thinkers is just misspent energy and time. Let this conflict be as it is because we need not take any one side of these extreme views of the traditional conservatives of either the East or the West. But still the view that the method of faith and intuition in Philosophy mostly followed in East is the only practicable, useful and trustworthy way; As knowledge is neither Western nor

Eastern, but universal. It is also not true that the Eastern Philosophers abrogated reason as absolutely futile, though they emphasised its natural limits. There are certain Philosophical schools in the East too, which establish their systems exclusively on rational grounds without discrediting the value and need of intuition in any way.

The great Philosopher Acharya Sankara, who was an ardent adherent to authority and revelation, made full use of the powers of logical reasoning in founding his stupendous system and said that the vedanta is ornamented by the fact that its strength lies not merely in appealing to authority and revelation but by reason and experience also. He however adds a note that reason unbridled which goes counter to revelation should be rejected as misleading.

Anyhow we can make use of methods and conclusions of the systems of the west to a certain extent only in gaining mastery over the Philosophies of the Eastern seers and sages.

The Philosophy of the Sanatana Method (Vedanta) is Characterised by integrality in its meaning, method and scope; built on the foundations of the most incisive, fully consistent logical analysis and it rejects nothing as totally useless, though it accepts nothing without sifting it through the seive of direct experience in super-sensuous intuition. The special feature of the Sanatana Method is that it is not opposed to any philosophical or speculative school, but accepts each at a particular stage in the evolution of the human consciousness. Keeping in view the above said nature of True Philosophy I have tried to present a critical estimate of the prominent modern Philosopher of the West–Immanuel Kant (1724-1804 A.D.) by pointing out how far the Universal Philosophy (Vedanta, i.e. the Sanatana method of Philosophy) agrees or disagrees western thoughts and especially the Kantian thoughts.

To begin with as we have discussed about the nature of a true philosophy, it is necessary to define such a philosophy, which is dealt in the next chapter.

2

The True Definition of a True Philosophy

Philosophy is a well coordinated and systematic attempt to evaluate life and the Universe as a whole, in reference to first principles that underlie all things as their causes and are implicit in all experience. It is an impartial approach to all problems and aspects of life, existence and knowledge. Its studies are not devoted merely to this Empirical Physical world, as Science does. It does not restrict itself to faith, authority and/or to the questions of the other world, just like Theology. It does not confine itself to the investigation of mind and its behaviour, like Psychology. It does not just deal with causistry or ethology like Moral Science and Ethics. It does not consider only the matters related to civic duties, problems of administration and constitution, as done in Political Science. It is not only concerned with the solution of the problems and techniques of adjusting, ordering and discovering the origin, organisation and development of Human Society as is done in Economics and Sociology. But Philosophy is adopted for an exhaustive treatment of the basic presuppositions "key concept" of each and everyone of these, that on which all these are ultimately founded and which forms the base of all knowledge and experience in general.

Philosophy investigates the very possibility and conditions of knowledge, its extent, nature and value. It depends on facts already known and rises above them to absolute varieties, on which all phenomena depend and by which they can be rationally explained. It is not confined or restricted by the limitations of the past, present and future, by the laws of any place or country; but refers to all times, places and conditions. It includes in itself all branches of learning and acts as a touchstone to all other aspects of human knowledge. Philosophy is a rational enquiry into the forms, content and implications of experience. It is an attempt to attain the complete knowledge of being in all the phases of its manifestation in the various evolution processes of consciousness. It is the discovery of the ultimate meaning and essence of the existence. It is the art of perfect life, the science of reality, the foundation of the practice of righteousness and the law for the attainment of absolute total bliss. Philosophy is the consummation of knowledge, the sacred love of the eternal, the methodology of the ascent of the finite to the infinite and finally it is the way to the knowledge of being as it is.

Therefore Philosophy is not just love for wisdom or striving for wisdom, but it is a moral and intellectual science which tries to explain the reality behind appearances by reducing the phenomena of the universe to ultimate causes by the application of reason and law. Thus the goal of Philosophy is in the highest generalisation conceivable, and this depends on the final grasping of the deepest meaning of the existence as a whole. It is not constructed only by the higher purified intellect of man but is revealed by intuition and is meant to justify rationally one's faith in Truth. Philosophy does not evolve by sensual experiences and/or by unaided abstract intellect but it is revealed by the intellect free from all desires, purged of all prejudices and based on immediate supersensual intuition. Hegel accepts this view to a certain extent only and not completely in his work 'Philosophy of Religion'as follows— "Philosophy is not a wisdom of the world, but is knowledge of what is not of the world; it is not knowledge which concerns external mass or empirical existence and life; but is knowledge of that which is eternal, of what God is, and what flows out of His nature."

The supreme purpose of Philosophy is not circumscribed by the contents of empirical experience but extends to the final and uncontradicted attainment of the Absolute by pure intuitional experience. Therefore Philosophy is the expression of the inner urge to know the Absolute. It is the way, not simply explaining what ought to be, but of directly experiencing that which eternally exists. It is the pursuit of reality. It is spiritual realisation expressed in logical language, while passing through the mill of Reason. Thus, Reason is just like a hand-maid to the higher intuition, used to proclaim the truth and value of intuition in the world of sense perception. It means that a purely intellectual Philosophy can never discover reality, for this discovery is possible only through supersensory intuition and not by any other means. It is absolutely and totally impossible to produce a perfect Philosophy through the instrumentality of reason alone and or by any other means of perception other than intuition, because Reason depends on the awareness of duality and on the concept of dichotomy (continuous division into pairs) of existence whereas truth is non-duality. Therefore there is no similarity between the characteristics of Reason and the Nature of Reality.

Philosophy can never explain Truth as it is, it cannot even pretend to do so but it can only intimate us about the existence of a supersensible absolute being which is manifesting in each and every experience of ours as their true value, essence and justification, as the highest consummation and bliss of all individuals in the universe. Philosophy is a necessary means for experiencing this higher knowledge of Self.

If Philosophy is defined as a process of the function of the intellect, then we have to note that it is not always the sole means; for Philosophy does not only impress the intellect of man, but it pierces the heart and feelings as well. Therefore it is not enough to understand the teachings of Philosophy, it is necessary to feel them in the depths of the heart. Feeling, in certain aspects surpasses understanding although feeling is strengthened often by understanding. Feeling is not just being emotional. True feeling begins when one transcends emotions. Thus Philosophy is an intensely practical science.

Philosophy has its roots in the practical needs of man. When man is content with the minimum requirements of his worldly life then he wants to know about transcendental matters, especially when he is in a reflective state. There is an urge within everyone to know about the secret of Birth and Death, the secret of Immortality, the nature of the Soul, etc...

Philosophy is the general exposition of the ultimate concepts, meanings and values of the things of the universe and also of the Being that pervades the universe, by reaching up to their final causes which range beyond the reach of the sense too. It is only Philosophy that can concern itself to the metaphysical essences by resting on the strong foundation of the testimony given by sages through deep meditation and realization. Therefore the source as well as aim of Philosophy is direct, non-mediate, supersensory and super logical experience.

All knowledge that we usually obtain in this world is mediatory and sensory, for it requires the operation of the triune process of the knower, knowledge and the known. By this method of knowing, it is not possible to acquire a faultless pure knowledge of Reality, for mediacy in knowledge does not enjoy the characteristics of permanency as it is not 'direct'. The transitory nature of mediate knowledge affects the whole world of science because science is bound by senses which again rely on physical instruments like microscope, telescope etc... There are many hypothetical conceptions and principles which are absolutely necessary to obtain scientific knowledge, (I am using the word science here in the sense in which it is understood by scientists today) and there are the notions and concepts of the existence of an outwardly extended space, of a flowing time and of the presence of material objects extending outside consciousness. In other words, Science is a co-ordinated and systematised knowledge of the contents of the world as it is observed through the physical senses of men. Science actually lays too much trust in the validity of some perception and thus gets vitiated by the gross limitations of the senses.

Philosophy works above empiricality, though it takes the help of empirical concepts and categories for proclaiming to the world the truths experienced by intuition. It speaks to the world in the language of the world, because the language of intuition cannot be grasped by the intellect of the world. The form and shape of Philosophy depends essentially on the stuff out of which the world of experience is made, on account of its having to perform the function of transmitting the knowledge of the super mundane ideals to the realm of mundane values. It has always within itself a living undercurrent of significance and implication which gives a vivid picture of the nature of the ultimate to the understanding mind. Thus in the beginning Philosophy stands on the shoulders of the senses, but later looks beyond them. For,

Intuition is the soul of Philosophy and Reason its body. By intuition, again, I do not mean the sensory intuition of certain Western philosophers; but the integral intuition of consciousness, which is non-different from the absolute, as accepted by the pioneers of Eastern Philosophy. Philosophy gives us a majestic magical vision of the illusory world based on the Absolute, as if, it was a manifestation of Absolute.

What is True Philosophy?

A True Philosophy is that which leads an aspirant to experience Absolute Knowledge as reality which is again consciousness and bliss as one, i.e., non-dual Absolute. Therefore knowledge of reality is not just an Idea but an immediate realization of the Eternal presence, which is absolute consciousness, bliss and pure knowledge as non-dual. Such an Absolute is necessary for the existence of the world, but the world is not necessary for the existence of the Absolute. Because again existence is itself Absolute. The undifferentiatedness and transcendence of qualities with its names and forms do not in any way mean reducing reality to non-being or abstract. Though what is true in the world is the underlying Absolute alone, the name and forms are illusory. Therefore an aspirant has to carefully distinguish between the gross concept of the world and the true concept of it. A purified analytic mind of the aspirant decides that the world is only a conglomeration of isolated abstract names and forms, which, when are totally isolated from Absolute loose all reality. A common man's untrained non-analytic mind confuses about what is the permanent element in what we call the world as full of abstract appearances, which are merely accidental. Therefore it is wrong to think that world is a real permanence and the absolute as abstract. The truth is just the reverse. The misapprehension is due to a false perception of the true relation of Reality to appearance. In the Absolute, all the physical, mental, moral, aesthetic, spiritual and all other aspirations of individuals find their true consummation, and hence Absolute cannot be abstract. Though the world is relative to perception but still its goal is Absolute, what the senses perceive is but the outer changing mode of the fact of the relativity of experience. On a careful critical analysis of the nature of the world it is found to fade away into nothingness until only consciousness remains.

The well-known Scientist Eddington has perfectly remarked that—the Scientists have chosen the world's solid substance from the continuous liquid to the atom, from the atom to the electron and there they have lost it. That means to say what science has abrogated is not reality but appearance, and after everything is said, there remains the irreducible substratum of the consciousness of Self. Because the Self is beyond the province of science, mind and intellect; and the scientists who have reached the boundaries of knowledge have discovered the limitations of reason only while careful observation forces everyone to accept Reality. This is actually what has happened and great scientists have either given imitations of that something about which science is not able to say anything or are totally silent. Hence the True Philosophy proclaims that the super-sensuous basis of this world (matter and energy, space and time, etc...) is the non-dual secondless one real Absolute.

What is Integral Intuition?

Kant and most of the Western Philosophers accept sensual or intellectual intuition and not non-sensuous integral intuition. One has to understand the difference between these two types of intuitions.

Most of our perceptions and percepts are governed by the characters of our sensibility and understanding. Actually it is "What We are" that greatly affects our ways of knowing and understanding. Thus, we cannot agree with Kant that Philosophical pursuits should be given up altogether as specimens of a vain enterprise on the part of man because the character of senses and mind differs from man to man. Kant, concerning himself too much with individual powers of knowledge, tries to dispense with the metaphysics of an ultimate reality as something totally impossible. Kant's contention is that, as knowledge is limited to the perceptual categories of the sensibility and the conceptual categories of the understanding, even our knowledge of God is impossible.

Yes, we cannot have a satisfactory metaphysics of reality if sense and reason are our sole aid. For, it is true that knowledge we attain is empirical and limited, being confined to the categories of the sensibility and understanding; from which no one can extricate himself. Therefore, as sensuous intuition also falls into the same category even it cannot give us conclusive results. But this problem does not arise in the Philosophy of the saints of the East. To them Philosophy is the embodiment in reason of the integral intuitional wisdom of Truth as it is. Because Absolute is not a thing which can be coloured by the functions of the senses and the understanding, as it is not dependent on senses and understanding for its existence like the world. But it is the very presupposition of the senses, understanding and reason. I would like to re-emphasise here that Philosophy is not the achievement of the unaided reason walking independently over the non-dualistic intuition, but is only the rational articulation of the super-rational realised in the realms of Integral intuition. God, freedom, immortality, etc... are not objects of unaided pure reason, which reason has to establish independently; but represent the highest goal which reason has to justify basing itself on the experience of the sages as stated in the Upanishads. To Kant, metaphysical realities are only regulative principles, but cannot be justified by reason. But to the Sages of the East, this is so only when reality is bifurcated into the objects of reason and of sensory intuition and not taken as one whole. But when reason draws inspiration from non-sensory experience and breathes the air of integral intuition, then what it declares is not merely a regulative principle, instead it represents what is real in the highest sense. Therefore the Reality that is established by philosophy has to be experienced in the state of deep meditation, where consciousness and Being become one. This is not any type of communion but it is just being it. Thus there is no such a thing as subject—object—relationship in regard to the universal consciousness. A person either experiences it fully in non-dualistic communion or does not know it at all. The senses, understanding and reason are powerless instruments in an attempt at perfectly comprehending its nature or realizing it in the form of experience; Because in the realization of the Supreme Being (the absolute super non-dual consciousness) the mind of the individual is completely transcended, together with all its dualistic categories.

The mind does not have any of the characteristics of the Reality. It is not conscious and also not universal in nature. It is a feeble objective insentient evolute acting as the individual's instrument in the perception of the external world, which is physical in nature. By its very nature it knows only what is in contact with it or what is presupposed by it. Hence anything that is known to the human being within this empirical world can be of no use in the realm of trans-empirical consciousness. The objects of the senses get fused, as it were, in the constitutive essence of the Absolute; space, time and causation, matter, energy and objects vanish in the light of its stupendous experience. The Absolute discussed in philosophy is not an object of consciousess, but is what consciousness itself is in its real and essential nature. Thus integral intuition in philosophy is the only pathway to the realization of the absolute consciousness through the different stages of the relative consciousness.

The Nature of Non-Sensuous Integral Intuition

This type of intuition is not mental or intellectual and not even of a mystical type but it is metaphysical. For, intuition is the direct apprehending act of consciousness. It is that power experienced in the higher realm of mind which perceives the truth of things immediately, independent of sensation, reasoning, induction and deduction or any other type of mediacy. Thus intuition is the non-mediate apprehension by a subject of its own essence, of the reality of its conscious states, of other minds, of other objects in the world, or of abstract universals. It transcends all mediacy (senses, mind, intellect, reason, etc.) and constitutes the full blossoming of all lower faculties into perfection. Remember! intuition is not inspiration. The former is knowledge in its totality of the known while the latter is just a mental experience caused by the transmission of qualities from a higher consciousness to the mind.

Intution is an active awareness of the immortal and blissful Self within. It is the eye by which anyone can experience even the abstract like things—the all pervading, self-luminous, Soul, Pure Reality. This, the touch stone of Philosophy. This is the only method of discerning the truth to attain self-Realization. This is the ultimate source of all proofs of knowledge. All other instruments of knowledge-sense perception, inference, verbal testimony, etc., give us only an indirect knowledge. The highest and perfect direct revealation comes to the Self by itself alone, independent of external instruments (including the internal-organ) and all other accessories needed in empirical knowledge. The deepest secrets of Nature and innermost essence of the beingness of the universe can be known only in intuition in which no process is involved, but the beingness of the object known is experienced as the existence content of consciousness. Because, the immediacy of intuitive perception is different from the apparent non-mediacy of sense-perception. Knowledge in the working and dream states is knowledge by process, requiring a relation between the knower and the known. But in intuition the object of knowledge does not exist outside as something alien to it. It gets assimilated into the constitution of knowledge itself just like dream. By intuition we are assured of the inner meaning, inner essence and significance of things, of a supernatural import in the sutructure of the universe and its cause-Nature and/or Ignorance too. Thus intuition is also of different grades depending upon the essence of the object known. The highest form of intuition is the recognition of the Self by itself in all things, recognising all things as super-imposed manifestation of itself and thus non-duality of itself. In the scriptures four major stages have been discussed. They are as follows: 1. God dwelling in all things. 2. All things are in God. 3. All things are God. And so finally, 4. I am God, the Pure Self, the Absolute Reality. Thus **plato** has said rightly—intuition is a conversation of the soul with itself.

Certain experiences are often called as Intuition, though they are rather inspirations than true intuition. The creative power of the unconscious mind is such that sometimes the rational activity of the mind goes on below the sub-liminal level. It can continue far below the threshold of consciousness, in sleep and dream, very often. The mind yields ready forms of ratiocination and solutions. The activity of the higher mind is an unconscious functioning of the expression of the soul at the background of every mental function. The workings of the mind do not permit conscious willing except in the limited form in which they manifest, and they brook no encroachment by even reason. But intuition as developed in the spiritual field widens the scope of reason and makes conscious willing possible in the highest degree, and in every direction. In the lower form of intuition a supersensory process of perception may make a superficial distinction between the Knower and the Known. But this distinction is without much difference, for this knowledge distinction is really something like the difference observed between the different parts or/and a practical distinction between the knower and known, but the fact of the assimilation of the existence of the object into knowledge abolishes in intuition all real distinction, in kind or characteristic. Whereas in the higher forms of intution even this flow of knowledge towards an object ceases, for here the object is known in its true nature, as ultimately one with the consciousness. This is what happens in the intuition of the Absolute.

As seen before there is a lot of difference between *inspiration, lower forms of intuition* and *higher forms of intuition;* Similarly there is a lot of difference between *intellectual intuition* and *supersensuous intution,* for, there is a very big difference between intellect and intuition itself. Because In intellectual analysis truth is distorted and falsified to some extent, for here existence gets separated into the subject and the object. Without duality there is no intellectual function, and with duality there can be no knowledge of Reality. The intellect breaks up the unity of being into a system of isolated terms and relations. The predicate is differentiated from the subject and then dovetailed into the subject itself by being made an adjective of the latter. The unitary existence is thus divided into a primary and a secondary aspect, which causes false perception. Whatever be the extent of the predicate of a logical proposition, it cannot be more than empirical knowledge, for it is the knowledge by division and not union of the subject and the object. An aggregate of an infinite number of particulars cannot give us the knowledge of the Absolute. Sense, feeling, thought and understanding, together with violation, are all below the level of intuition. In all physical process, knowledge takes the form of an artificial relation of the predicate to the subject; but in intuition there is no adjectual predicate required to qualify the subject, for it is knowledge of existence in essence. Actually Man's powers of knowledge are not adopted to comprehend Reality. For, one's consciousness had adapted itself to understanding the world in terms of time and space. If it were freed from keeping busy with the perception of the outer world and focussed upon a world of 'noumenon', it would transcend time and space and adopt itself to preceiving the noumenon in a special way. It is intuition alone that is capable to grasp the various particulars and categories together to form a harmonious whole and enable the Self to enter the portals of Reality.

But, Intellect and intuition are not really opposed to each other. Because, intellect is lifted up and universalised in the purified state of intuition. *Intuition does not negate intellectual* perception but *transfigures it into a higher quality* of perception. the purpose of intellect is fulfilled in the illumination of the intuition. What intellect activates is only understanding, while that which is gained by intellect in intuition is practical wisdom. the intellect functions on the wrong basis of the assumption that the results achieved by the process of the distinction between the knower and the known are fully trustworthy. Without belief in this difference there can be no logic, and with this difference there is no truth or reality. The complete synthesis of true knowledge would be a union of principles where the intellect is overcome, where reason lies above itself, and where differences re obliterated. Until and unless a person is not dissatisfied with his low level of human consciousness, he cannot achieve this type of pure knowledge. But the moral urge in everyone to reach perfection, to attain liberation, points to the existence of some such knowledge which is not limited in any way. This aspiration can be fulfilled only in non-mediate experience of Self by the super-sensuous intuition.

In matters transcendental, such as the existence of God, the unity of the world and its illusory property, the immortality of the Soul, non-duality, etc., the pronouncements of the intellect can never be free from the defects of wrong notion and doubts, for it is rooted in duality. Similarly, either deductive logic or inductive logic and neither unaided pure reason nor discursive reason cannot reach the portals of reality, for they are concerned with objects that are imagined outside the Self and are externally related to knowledge. Thus, senses, mind, intellect and reason, all in their search of truth will always have to be guided by the deliverance of intuition; for it is the nature of these to move along the edge of a precipice through which they usually fall into an error, which finally proves their own ruin. On the contrary, Intuition in its highest reaches is not knowledge *of* Being but knowledge *as* Being. Self knowledge is the summit of intuitive perception, which is in-separable from self-existence.

But never misunderstand the highest intuition to be self-knowledge or self-knowledge to be a product of intuition. As, self-knowledge is the only true and direct knowledge. All else is rational, mediate, inferrential and presupposes the characteristics of knowledge as attained in intuition. For, it is the light of the self that flashes forth and overshadows all knowledge that are acquired by man in this world. The possibility of such intuition and intuitive knowledge is demonstrated in the metaphysical acceptance of the Absoluteness of the Self. But we should never equate Self-Realization with intuition or intuitive knowledge in the sense of any kind of perception, even if it be the highest perception, for Self-Realization, is *being* itself.

Intuition gives an entire and concrete insight into Reality, while the intellect gives partial knowledge abstracted from reality. Intuition reveals the cosmic interrelatedness of things before revealing Reality, while intellect gives a static picture of isolated objects. Intuition gives a synthetic view of Reality, while intellect provides us with analytic concepts of falsely bifurcated entities. The intuition of Reality is, verily, omniscience, and omniscience is at once omnipotence. This is to attain the existence, knowledge and freedom in their completeness. As the essence of Man is truth and not error, error is an aberration from one's own *Being*. Thus, the law of perfection, in general, is in relation to and in consonance with the inner perfection of the individual. So, the individual and the universe are not two Realities, but one in their substratum.

Inspiration, revelation, insight, intuition, ecstasy, divinesight and supreme bliss are the seven planes of knowledge. There are four sources of knowledge—instinct, reason, intuition and super-intuition. Instinct is seen in birds, animals plants, and illiterate mundane people. Reason is higher than instinct and is found only in human beings, wherein the ego interferes with the divine-play. For, it collects facts, generalises, reasons out from cause to effect and vice-versa, from premises to conclusions, from propositions to proofs. It concludes, decides and gives judgment. Intuition (mental or intellectual) is better than reason, for, it takes one safely to the door of non-sensuous intuition; As pure reason leads towards Intuiton. The non-sensuous intuition leads to direct perception of Truth. Things are known with their essence by a flash. So this type of intuition transcends intellectual intuition and pure-reason both, but never contradicts them until and unless they are not against Reality. The knowledge of the limitations of reason and intellectual intuition is an acceptance of there being a knowledge transcending both of them. Because a knowledge of things within certain limits of boundary, implies the knowledge of what is beyond that limit or boundary. The inspiration for infinite knowledge and the urge for perfection, total peace, total freedom, absolute bliss, etc... points out to an experience of its supremacy over all things known to man. That experience is none-other than the knowledge of Self, also called as Super-Intuition. Once this has been attained, the one will feel Absolute by its ownself in the objects of the universe. The knowledge of truth is itself perfected knowledge which is the non-dual, existence, consciousness-bliss form of oneself. Thus intuition (super) is the Golden key to the blissful blessedness. By such a super intuition which is called as Integral intuition in the Sanatana Method one gets relieved from ignorance and settles in oneself. This is liberation.

Is Philosophy an Experience?

Philosophy is not to be confused with intuition, with mystic or religious experience only; though these are very powerful aids in achieving the experience of Pure Reality. Philosophy in the East is based on the revelations of the sages and provides necessary strength to mankind for realizing his goal. In mystic and religious experience the intellect and the reason are completely transcended, while Philosophy is all intellect and reason; though its aim is deep religious experience. While the intuitional truths are rationally explained by philosophy, it does not even pretend to prove the nature of these truths through intellectual or scientific categories. Because Philosophy has a negative value of offering an exhaustive criticism of sense experience and logical thought, indirectly arriving at the concept of reality by demonstrating the limitations and inadequacies of the former. All Philosophy really springs from an inward dissatisfaction with immediate empirical experience and a profound study of its hidden implications. This is Philosophy.

A justification of super-mental and non-temporal Absolute is attempted through a searching analysis and understanding of sense-experience and rational judgement, while the defects and implications of the latter are fully disclosed. Truly speaking, Philosophy can neither be purely subjective to its approach nor objective in the sense of an alienation from the perceiving subject. It will be seen in the critical analysis of the principles constituting the universe that—what is implied within the experience is also implied outside in the contexts of experience, i.e., the objects and the conditions that are necessary for bringing out this experience. Thus, Philosophy becomes an universal approach to truth made by the subject and the object simultaneously with equal authority, meaning and strength, making no difference in value between themselves. The movement of thought is from the physical to the biological, from the biological to the logical and finally from the logical to the spiritual. Philosophy should therefore constitute a comprehensive analysis and study of the whole of experience. It has no potentialities, no prejudicies, no preconceptions, no dislikes and no likes, and therefore not a dogma. It moves unbridled with truth, justice and wisdom as its supreme aims. It makes ample use of all the powers that the human being is endowed with and reaches the farthest limits of these powers, where what it observes and studies is not that which is immediately experienced; but what is inferred from and implied logically in the facts it envisages directly in that borderland between understanding and reason. Man possesses nothing superior to Reason, and so science cannot go beyond it. On the other hand, Philosophy is a rational criticism of reason itself, when we take reason to mean not merely an isolated abstract power of intelligence, but also all the objective factors and conditions that are necessary to make it what it is. When reason rationally knows it's own limitations and the reason why it is limited, then it knows reality in a negative way. This negative knowledge becomes the starting point of the effort towards its positive realisation in meditation.

Philosophy has no opposition or contradiction or enemity with science or any other means of modernisation. It concedes that science is necessary and useful in reinforcing its own conclusions; but it strictly warns science that it is limited to physical phenomenon. Thus it does not extend to the aim or goal of life. We study the physical, chemical and biological laws in Science, the logical and metaphysical principles in philosophy, the moral and the spiritual varieties in Religion and Higher Mysticism too. The senses, reason and intuition are our means of knowledge in the progressive unfoldment of our nature and self. Science, Philosophy and Mysticism are all true and useful in their own places and together they constitute the highway-road to the knowledge of life. Intuition, however, has the special advantage of being able to unfold all that the sense and reason can know, and in addition, also all that these cannot even hope to know with all their power. Therefore Philosophy which is an outcome of a pure non-sensuous intuition is a means to experience the reality as experience in itself but Science is not so.

Classifications in Philosophy

To understand Philosophy properly, nowadays (as per modern view) it has been classified into seven (7) major divisions. They are as follows: Metaphysics, Epistemology, Ethics, Psychology, Axiology, Mysticism and Aesthetics.

Metaphysics

Philosophy concerned as metaphysics deals with an extensive reasoned discussion of the natures and the relations of God, World and the Individual Soul. The latter two are either identical in essence with God, or are totally different from God. The ultimate Reality is either God or the world of perception alone or only the individual mind. God either exists or not, and is necessary or unnecessary for an explanation of experience. The world is either material or mental in nature; and it is either independent of Consciousness or dependent on matter; the world is either pluralistic or a single whole; and is real or unreal; empirial, pragmatic or rational. The individual is free or bound, etc... Questions of this nature are usually discussed under metaphysics. It also delineates (explains) the process of cosmogony (the theory of creation of universe) and cosmology (the science of universe); the concepts of space, time and causation, creation, evolution and involution, as well as the presuppositions of eschatology or the discourse on the nature of life after death. Therefore the Philosophical basis of Modern Physics and Biology also can be comprised under metaphysics.

Epistemology

Under this branch of Philosophy the various theories and processes of the acquisition of right knowledge, as well as the nature and possibility of wrong knowledge are discussed in detail. Sensation, perception, inference, comparison, verbal testimony, presumption, non-apprehension and non-rational intuition are the various phases of the means of Right Knowledge. Intuition, however, should not be classified as one of the instruments of objective knowledge like senses, for it is the only supreme means of right knowledge, transcending all other empirical means which have their own limitations. Knowledge of one thing when mistaken to be of another is most erroneous, whatever the reason be for the error. Therefore, the several causes of error in perception are also discussed in epistemology to get rid of ones perception.

Ethics

This branch of Philosophy engages itself in the ascertainment of the nature of right and wrong, good and bad. It also deals with the moral-standards and moral-judgements; the rights and the duties of the individual, the society and the state, the national and international good, the nature and function of conscience, etc... Therefore, Ethics is either naturalistic, hedonistic or metaphysical.

Psychology

Under this branch the constitution, function and behaviour of mind is discussed in detail. Psychology, apart from its dealing with general topics, such as -the springs of action, thought, intelligence, emotion, will, feeling, the relation of mind and body, the nature of internal conflict, the mechanism of sense knowledge, etc... It may also be distinguished as to deal with the individual, social, educational, religious, analytic and group psychology.

Axiology

Philosophy under Axiology establishes the nature of values in the different stages and views of life, such as—physical values, aesthetic values, moral values, religious values, etc.

Aesthetics

Under this branch of Philosophy we deal wih the significance and the nature of beauty which is either subjective or objective or relative to the subject and the object. It also deals with such things which is either real or ideal or unreal and other related matters.

Mysticism

This is the most important and magnificent part of Philosophy. Though certain rationalists, in their enthusiasm of saving themselves from falling into irrationalism of any kind, commit the error of not knowing that the Pure Mysticism actually deals with truths that range beyond and determine all rational processes of knowledge. Mysticism mostly concerns with inner relation of the individual to the eternal being and with the various techniques of the ascent of the soul in the fulfilment of its religious and spiritual aspiration, with the picturesque experiences it undergoes and the dangers and difficulties it has to encounter on the way. It also deals with the psychology of the phenomenon of religious consciousness as well as the physical foundations and implications of the inner path of the Spirit. It also accounts for the meditations which a seeker of truth has to practice for the ultimate experience to attain pure reality.

Philosophy is a term generally applied to a study of all these aspects of life's meaning, and so it forms the most attractive pursuit of the human being.

Thus we have discussed about the nature and a true definition of a true philosophy, but still, it is necessary to know about the need of a philosophy. Otherwise it is not possible to make a modern man realise the importance of philosophy in life, for this let us proceed and discuss it in the next chapter.

3

The Need of a Philosophy

All persons live in accordance with their own philosophy of life that they have framed for themselves, consciously or unconsciously. Even the uneducated and the uncultured have a rough and ready philosophy of their own. Therefore, life without a philosophy is unimaginable. Thus, Philosophy is generally defined as love for wisdom or the knowledge of things in general up to their ultimate causes, so far as reason can attain to such a knowledge. It is a comprehensive and critical study or analysis of experience as a whole. Whether it is consciously, deliberately or rationally adopted on conviction or unconsciously followed in life through faith or persuasion, every man constructs for himself a fundamental philosophy as the basis of life, a theory of the relation of the world and the individual, which shapes his whole attitude to life. It is only when we confine the concept of philosophy to the laboured edifices of academic men that we are forced to say that only a few in the world study or understand and have a philosophy in their life. Even those who deliberately say that there is no need of any philosophy also have a hidden secret philosophy of their own. They do have a theory of reality, though it may consist only in denying it altogether. They also have a rough theory of the world, though it may be only one of cross material conception or of a superstitious belief in the supremacy of some personalities and forces of myth and fable.

We have an ethics, an epistemology and even a logic of our own; though it may be a purely personal or limited to a group of persons of kindred ideas and temperaments. Under these conditions it is certainly advisable to the intellectuals to frame a systematic and intelligent philosophy for the life of all, after critically examining and understanding the nature of the world and our experiences in it. And if we consistently carry on sincere efforts with critical intelligence within logical limits, then we will find that philosophies are not propounded personal theories but are universal and they form a science and also an art of human life taking towards completeness. Surely at that stage we will arrive at a philosophy not of this or that school, but a philosophy of humanity in general. We would reach to a most liberal, broad minded, universal, flexible and tolerant theory of the universe and its contents, acceptable to all men of reason without any prejudice. A universal Philosophy based on experiences that are common to all human beings of the world could be easily framed.

Difficulties and problems arise due to our definitions of experience or of the limits we set to it or of the authoritativeness in it. We may limit Philosophy to sense experience, to understanding, to reason or to intuition. To speak frankly, it is true that intution is the only instrument that enjoys the greatest universality of scope and drives deepest into the mysteries of existence. Therefore a perfect philosophy is that which springs out of non-sensory integral intuition of Reality.

Even though some western philosophers have described the constitution of Philosophy as an expression of a certain attitude, purpose and temper of conjoint intellect and will, The Eastern philosophers add intuition as forming the foundation of the functions of the intellect and will, which usually work with the material supplied by the senses.

Philosophy is a complete world view and a general attitude of intellect, will and feeling to life. It gives an explanation of the universe at large, by appealing to what is discoverable at the deepest of known facts. It is not a mere description of the bits or details of any physical observation. We call an explanation as philosophical when it is broad enough to be harmoniously related to the other views of life and fulfils the needs of all the faculties of man to the highest degree of satisfaction, using ultimate universal principles and not mere empirical facts, in establishing its validity.

According to **William James**— "Philosophy is a compendious name for the spirit in education." It is only in this true sense of the process of the education and unfoldment of the spiritual sport in man that "Philosophy" is worth its name. To teach a doctrine in a dogmatic and forced way is one thing, and to do it in a rational and appealing way in its greatness and fullness is another. The latter is the taste and the way of philosophy. Its value in imparting true culture to man, to make him wise and useful to both himself and to others is inestimable. Even according to Kant, philosophy wakes us from our "dogmatic slumber" and makes us critical in our outlook, opening before us the majesty and reality of the unknown, giving us strength to stand firm and assert our rightful citizenship of the universe. Our whims, fancies and prejudices are broken, and philosophy makes us free and liberal in our attitudes. The Philosopher is raised above the usual clinging to immediate practical needs and is enabled to roam fearlessly in the Emperean of the joy springing from within. This is what a true philosopher achieves when he gains access to reality, and it is not available to those who are sunk in earthliness, i.e., materialism, bound by material urges and content with what they have attained by senses, reason and understanding only.

Science and Philosophy

To press the need of a philosophy it is necessary to realize the difference between modern science and philosophy. Because it is often said that philosophy is not useful as science, that science has made much progress while philosophy is lagging behind and that science has optimum utility while philosophy has none. This type of complaint come mostly from materialistic minded partial observers who are just looking into the strides of science which is making many inventions that save our labour, time and money and these make our daily life comfortable. But, this of which man boasts of so much is "Applied Science" and not science as such in its true sense, which scientists call as "Pure Science". When a man fails to know how to use the time saved by him due to applied science, and how to spare time to do what is really solacing to him in his busy mechanical life, for this Science has no answer. We ask science to clearly show where and of what use is of this advanced science in attaining pure knowledge. Also look into the morality of man today, and of what civilisation and culture he has been endowed by science and its applied form. Where comes the pride of applied science when selfishness, greed and jealousy are its masters? Is not science with its nuclear power threatening to make an end of man himself? See them whom science has tightened the knot that binds man to the prison-house of miseries raised by himself on the basis of belief in things that only tantalize him and then perish. I regret to mention that man has applied Science in his life and not Philosophy. And even where science is applied, it is done just like giving a sword in the hands of a child.

After a critical analysis of the present universe we can say that philosophy has really made more remarkable progress than science. How? Philosophy has tried to save man from the folly of ignorance and misconduct, raising him from the state of animalhood and blessing him with the light of love, service, sacrifice, etc. Finally philosophy has made man aware of the need for the dedication of the self to a purpose lifted above all human basic needs. Therefore the riches of science bereft of the wisdom of philosophy become distinctive possessions, fit to be feared and renunciated rather than be loved and adored. What fruits can one reap from scientific inventions without any moral, economical, political and administrative wisdom? Let not man pride himself over the advance of science because it has only invented tools without giving man the pure knowledge to use them properly for the good of humanity; thus these tools have become dreadful monsters without any wise-men to direct them with sagacity.

Science can describe the "how" of fragments of observation; but it is important to interpret and explain the meaning and value of what is observed—the "why" of visible phenomena. On the other hand philosophy does both and goes further, beyond sense observations too. Thus Philosophy is not a dry intellectual gymnastics. It is the wisdom of life reached after careful reflection and investigation, without which life is a dismal failure. Even the Western philosophers accept this as - **Socrates and Plato** emphatically pronounced the truth that— "those who lack right knowledge deserve to be stigmatised as slaves; Unless philosophers become kings or the existing kings acquire the genuine wisdom of philosophy and unless political power and philosophy is combined in one person, there will be no deliverance for cities, nor yet for the human race." This is an eternal truth which holds good for all times and climes. That is to say-- Administrators should first and foremost be philosophers in the true sense, not merely lovers but possessors of wisdom.

Renowned scientist, **Sir Arthur Eddington** has stated that our true personality and consciousness are not parts of observed phenomena. According to him, our deeper feelings are not of ourselves alone, but are glimpses of a reality transcending the narrow limits of the inferior consciousness. The stuff of the world is a limitless mind or consciousness. We know a particular world because it is that alone with which the consciousness interacts. He regards matter as a knowable substance grafted on a spiritual substratum. Reality is fundamentally spiritual and is general consciousness. He accepts that where science has progressed the farthest, it is nothing but the mind has regained from nature all that which it put into the nature by itself. At this juncture he has raised himself above physics and has entered the realms of philosophy and mysticism. This is what everyone of deep reflective thinking is obliged to do in the end. **Sir James Jeans** uses **Plato's** simile and says that science is just studying merely a reflection on the walls of the cave of a play that is being shown because of the sunlight entering in the cave. The substantiality as well as the objectivity of things is due to their subsistence in the mind of an eternal spirit. **Sir Bertrand Russell** says mind and matter are alike and are logical constructions, and the distinction between the psychical and the physical is not fundamental. The difference between mind and matter is not in their substance but in their function and arrangement. **Max Planck** does not think that consciousness can be explained in terms of matter and its laws. He regards consciousness as fundamental and matter as a derivative of consciousness. **Einstein** reverently contemplates the mystery of conscious life pertuating itself through all eternity and is content to try humbly to comprehend even an infinitesimal part of the intelligence manifested in nature. **R.A Milikan** says that a purely materialistic philosophy is the height of unintelligence. These scientists are clearly accepting that the absence cf the faculty of an intuitive perception of the divine presence is a kind of mental deficiency, which has been stated openly by Eddington. The great geniuses of science have felt the need for a higher study and experience than that provided to man by science.

The problem of causality has raised questions that stress the need for a philosophy. Science believes that every event has a cause and resort to a kind of linear argument *ad infinitum*, thinking that to be a cause means to be antecedent in time. Our movement from effects to causes leads us nowhere, and finally we find ourselves in a hopeless pursuit. The question of an ultimate cause cannot be answered by science. Because the end or purpose of action to it is enveloped in darkness. If the order and methods of events in the universe is determined, not by the way in which we are accustomed to observe cause and effect relation, but by the laws of a living organism directed by a unitary force; by such a postulation science will find itself in a fool's paradise. When there is mutual interaction among the constituents of the Universe, the commonsense view of causality collapses to the ground. To realize this properly we require a reflective study, which is provided by philosophy; by which we can come to a satisfactory conclusion regarding the true scheme of things. An enquiry into the nature of facts observed by science leads us to epistemology and metaphysics. It is impossible to desist anyone from working for the noble cause to which philosophy awakens us. Because the very denial of all possibility of knowing the nature of reality implies our rightful claim to know it. For that philosophy is the only source.

It is quite clear that there is no life without philosophy. Thus a true philosophy has to be brought out from the generalisation of the true experiences of human being. This is the need of the hour. For this a study of different methods of philosophy is necessary which is dealt in next chapter.

4

The Different Methods of Philosophy

A General View

The true philosophic method should not be lopsided, should not be biased to any particular or special dogma and should not be of prejudices. But it should comprehend within itself the processes of reflection and speculation and at the same time be able to reconcile the deductive and the inductive methods of reasoning. Thus, the methods employed in philosophical reasonings and enquiries include the basic presuppositions of scientific approach in general. Also, the philosophical processes endeavour to discover ways of considering and knowing the facts implied in the phenomena of experience.

Philosophy being the way of the knowledge of truth, its method must be in agreement with the nature of truth. In philosophy and religion, the end always determines the nature of the means. What we know is not entirely different in nature from the essential constitutions of the means by which we know it. The immediate objects of our experience here are the entities of the physical universe, and the means of our knowledge of them are our senses which are also of physical characteristics. Hence the method that philosophy employs in its approach to truth is much dependent upon what conception we have of philosophy and of the nature of the goal of philosophy.

Our goal may be matter, mind, spirit, or absolute. Accordingly we may become either materialists, idealists or mystics. Our instrument of knowledge may be the senses, understanding, reason or sensuous and intellectual intuition. Accordingly our theories of knowledge also lead us to be either empiricists, rationalists, transcendentalists, absolute idealists or spiritual intuitionists. All these theories resort mainly to two processes: 1. Contemplation of what is considered to be indubitable and real, and 2. A searching analysis with a critical study of empirical experience; including all the possible methods and conclusions of pure science. The former helps us to a greater knowledge of the goal of Philosophy while the latter to a disapproval of false values and vindication of the methods and fundamental principles of Philosophy. Therefore the theories of knowledge and reality, generally subject to a critical investigation as to their nature and contents, found strong systems of thought after protracted contemplation on the possible nature of Reality.

Before going into a discussion of the methods of Philosophy we have to give necessary attention to the principles laid down by the Philosopher **Descartes**. In his work "Discourse on Method", Descartes gives an outline of the process he followed in philosophical enquiry as follows:

"The *first* of these (principles) was to accept nothing as true which I did not clearly recognise to be so; that is to say, are fully to avoid precipitation and prejudices, and to accept in them nothing more than what was presented to my mind so clearly and distantly that I could have no occasion to doubt it. The *second* was to divide up each of the difficulties which I examined into as many as parts possible, and as seemed requisite in order that it might be resolved in the best manner possible. The *third* was to carry on my reflections on due order, commencing with objects that were the most simplest and easiest to understand; in order to rise little by little, or by degrees, to knowledge of the most complex; assuming an order even it be an imaginary one, among those which do not follow a natural sequence relatively to one another. The *last* was in all cases to make enumerations so complete and reviews so general that I should be certain of having omitted nothing."

Keeping in view these basic principles, let us see grossly the Sanatana Method of Philosophy. The Philosophy of the Absolute rises above all particulars to greater universals, basing itself on facts of observation and experience by the method of induction and gradual generalisation of truths, without missing even a single link in the chain of logic and argumentation, reflection and contemplation, until it reaches the highest generalisation of the Absolute truth; and thus by the deductive method comes down to interpret and explain the facts of experience in the light of the nature of Absolute Truth. This is the only most satisfactory method of philosophical enquiry.

Let us go through briefly on the different methods adopted by the West and the East.

Scepticism and Agnosticism

The marvel of creation evokes the admiration of man, and its mysteriousness excites his wonder; and this wonder naturally leads to a serious enquiry of things around. Because man is not content in a state of awe, based on ignorance, but is curious to know the truth behind the enthralling wonder of the world. He investigates, speculates, argues discusses and finally comes to a conclusion about the nature of things in this wonderful world. This becomes Man's Philosophy.

However, Modern man seems to have stepped into the region of philosophy through doubt and sceptical thinking. Man commenced doubting the validity of authority and dogma no less than that of accepted traditional beliefs. Descartes started with doubting everything, even the validity of thought itself. Later, Kant too followed the critical method of enquiry in Philosophy. Bradley also accepts for the need of sceptical study of the basic principles in philosophy. However, he adds: "By scepticism, it is not meant to doubt about or disbelief in some tenet or tenets. But, I understand it—an attempt to become aware of and to doubt all pre-conceptions". The technique of doubt in philosophical pursuits has the danger of the possibility of falling into the hopeless image of rank scepticism, with no ground for the denier or sceptic to stand on. Even Agnosticism, which is a smug way of coolly forgetting the basic significations of the sceptical outlook and speciously arguing that nothing definite can be known in reality.

Scepticism (technique of doubt) as a principle to be followed at the very beginning of the application of Methods of Philosophy is very essential; because, as above said, all Philosophy begins in wonder and doubt. An unknown and irresistible urge to know all about that which presents itself as something extending beyond the scope of human knowledge and a simultaneous dissatisfaction with the external view of things is the foundation of philosophy. Though philosophy may begin in doubt or wonder, it should not end in doubt, for then, the very purpose of philosophy is defeated. If the sceptic is left to confine himself to his position of universal doubt and disbelief then he becomes guilty of dogmatism. On the other hand if he tries to free himself from dogmatism, he cuts the ground from under his feet. This is the fate of sceptical approach which overreaches itself and stultifies its own purpose. We should thank **Descartes,** the acute, sincere and wise thinker for he detected this error in entertaining universal doubt and came to the wise condition that the existence of the doubter himself cannot be doubted. Thus, though his philosophy began with a doubt but ended in certainity. Scepticism as a method of philosophy has value only when it is accepted within its limitations and scope, and not when it tries to assume a metaphysical status.

Agnosticism is a natural consequence of the thorough going sceptical outlook, and it reaches the conclusion that the reality of things cannot be known, for almost the same reasons as those proclaimed by the sceptic. Knowledge of reality is impossible because we have no means to know it. It looks as if that the Agnostic position was in some way better than the findings of the sceptic, as the sceptic rejects all questions by disbelief out-rightly, due to his connection of there being no possibility of arriving any certainity regarding any thing, while the agnostic only denies the chance of our having any knowledge of it. But the theory as a whole is obviously untenable. Agnosticism as a method fails, because to assert that— "we know only appearance and cannot know any reality beyond it"—for this type of assumption we must already possess some knowledge of reality, without which we will not be able to have any distinction between appearance and reality. ***D.M. Edwards*** in his work "The Philosophy of Religion" states clearly— "Its essential defect is that it is based on the unconscious assumption that man is somehow an alien in the very world which gave him birth and in whose bosom he lives and moves and has his being, that he is doomed to look at the universe through the medium of forms and categories of thought which are mental spectacles of foreign fabrication". Even ***Bradley*** in his work " Appearance and Reality" states as follows—"To say that reality is such that our knowledge cannot reach it, is a claim to know reality; to urge that our knowledge is of a kind which always fails to transcend appearance, itself implies that transcendence is possible. For, if we had no idea of a beyond, we should assuredly not know how to talk about failure or success in reaching it. And the test, by which we distinguish them, must obviously be somehow in accquaintance with the nature of the goal."

Empiricism and Rationalism

Empiricism as a method of philosophy is mainly confined to sense experience. It urges that all knowledge obtained by the senses is of what is already existent outside themselves. Reason has its function only in carefully judging the nature of the perceptive material provided to it by the senses. Thus the laws of reasón according to empiricism are just copies of and controlled by knowledge which is a *posteriori*. *A priori* knowledge as accepted by rationalism in reason is totally impossible, because rational concepts are the byproducts of the experiential material. The source of knowledge is sense-experience only and not mind or reason. Therefore the method of acquiring knowledge is inductive. So ideas are reducible to sensations only. Knowledge cannot be gained by merely finding that the opposite of which is conceivable, as rationalism holds. Similarly truth cannot be established by the fact, that to, deny it implies, somehow, its reaffirmation. *A priori* knowledge independent of sense-experience is inconceivable. Therefore there are no universal and necessarily essential self-evident truths that are adumbrated (explained implicitly or explicitly) by rationalism. So is the conclusion of the Empiricists.

The defect of empiricism lies in the fact, that, the senses are untrustworthy as means of right-knowledge. Sense percepts have a little reality only in relation to the constitutions of the respective senses, and never independently. Minus the characteristics of the senses, our empirical concepts are nothing. That means, we know in an objective way only what is already contained in the very nature of senses subjectively. This is certainly not a reliable or valid right knowledge. The background of the sense-percepts are always unknown to us, and the attitude which we develop towards the *things-in-themselves* that lie beyond the reach of the senses is naturally doubtful. That means to say that we have to become sheer sceptics regarding the nature of reality. That is how **Locke's** empiricism paved the way for **Hume's** scepticism. The sceptic's attitude is very harmful for the progress of philosophy. If we are to carry scepticism to its logical limits, there can never be any such thing as universal and necessary truths. All that we know would be mere fragmentary and disconnected shreds of events. Such knowledge would convey no meaning at all, due to lack of causal relationship and necessary connection among themselves. Doubt and disbelief of every settled opinion is not only impracticable but is detrimental to the very position of the doubter. Because a true systematic doubter who seriously pursues his method without deceiving himself has to doubt his own judgments, in order that he may avoid the change of peremptoriness (having a doubtless final opinion) in his search for truth. This is what he cannot do. Therefore he doubts all other positions except his own. Such a dogmatic adherence to one's own convictions where other views are possible is not the characteristic of a true philosophical method. To know that 'we do not know' itself implies the acceptance of some criterion of certainity, some knowledge which we already possess without any trace of doubt. Truth, goodness and beauty—all lose their meaning and value when unconditional doubts sweep in. Then life becomes an empty affair, with no intellegible aim before it. Therefore, as empiricism is the precursor of scepticism, it is an incomplete and fallible method of enquiry into the nature of truth.

The **mathematical** method of **Rationalism** takes reason to be the sole means of acquiring philosophical knowledge. According to it, the objective universe is known, arranged and controlled by *a priori* laws of reason. The universe is an expression of the innate rational nature of the knowledgeable subject. The criterion of the truth is therefore not sensory but intellectual, rational and deductive. The mathematical methods of deductions are most suited to a proper method of philosophy. Knowledge is gained only when the opposite of the inconceivable is discovered. Truth can be established by the fact that to deny it implies its reaffirmation in one way or the other. Thus true knowledge is a priori and is independent of sense-experience. This knowledge is self-evident, and so it implies universal and necessary truths.

But even rationalism taken exclusively cannot escape the change of being non-critical in regard to its own position. How can the rationalist be sure that what he knows through his rational powers is uncontradicted knowledge? Because what one thinks to be a self-evident truth need not neccessarily be so for others. There is nothing, whatsoever, to prove that the principles which the rationalist logically deduces from his *a priori* concepts really correspond to the actual characteristics of the world of experience.

The **Geometrical** Method of **Rationalism** may be very pleasing to the philosophers, but even it has not won universal validity. The self evident nature of the truths discovered independently by rationalism has been questioned. Many of the so called truths are private to their owners and do not enjoy universal acceptance. Even in regard to the *principles of logic* and the *laws of thought,* there is no universal agreement. The rationalist is certain about the ability of reason to give him an uncontradiactable knowledge. He however forgets that reason cannot be taken as an infalliable instrument of knowledge and that its only function is critical examination, verification and judgement of the knowledge that we obtain through the senses.

Direct or immediate knowledge is acquired relatively in sense-perception and absolutely in intuitional revelation, but not in reason. Reason has a purely negative value and is not a positive means of knowledge. The senses and intuition provides us that knowledge which reason cannot contradict, though it can criticise and judge them. There are certain facts, of course, which we cannot even know through the senses; but this does not mean that reason can know them. It is only in spiritual intuition that they are realised. If a self-evident truth is confined to reason alone, its validity is capable of being doubted.

The Critical Method of Kant

The critical or transcendental method of philosophy introduced by Kant takes stock of the arguments of both empiricism and rationalism and builds up a new system. Kant follows the method of the analysis of the conditions and limits of knowledge. He points out that, though the material of our knowledge is supplied by the senses, the universality as well as the necessity about it comes from the very nature and constitution of the understanding, which is a faculty of the knower of all things in the world. But the world which we thus know through synthetic *a priori* knowledge is not the real world, for, it is built up by the materials supplied by the senses, which gain the characters of universality and necessity when they are brought into shape by the categories provided by the understanding. The world of reality cannot be known by the powers that man possesses at present. If we had been endowed with a consciousness-in-general or an intellectual intuition uninfluenced by the judgements and categories of the understanding, it would have been possible for us to know the reality as it is. What we know are just empirical facts or phenomena constructed by percepts and concepts common to all men. The postulates of reality that the reason advances are only necessities felt by it and are not realities in themselves.

In the philosophy of Kant' Reason reaches to it's highest limits and also becomes conscious of these limits. The strata of the sense, understanding and reason are thoroughly investigated and critically examined having their weaknesses exposed off well. All this is good. But Kant has actually discouraged all efforts in many matters, for ex-regarding the acquisition of knowledge of reality, making the very search for knowledge a hopeless affair etc. To him, knowledge is a synthetic relational product of the logical Self. He feels that the ideals of metaphysics on which the reason cherishes are just regulative principles which have no reality beyond being more hypotheses. He makes philosophy in the sense of metaphysics an impossibility, holding that all knowledge is phenomenal. One of the major defects of his system lies in his thinking that intuition is always confined to sense-perception, i.e., he accepts only a sensuous or intellectual intuition only. He feels that man can never have a non-mediate experience. Though he is profound enough to conceive of an intellectual intuition transcending the senses and understanding, yet still he does not raise it beyond a mere logical concept which does not share the nature of Reality. Though theoretically possible, his intellectual intuition has no practical value. The fact, however, appears to be that Kant was not aware that he himself had in him intimations of this intellectual intuition when he declared the world to be consisting of appearances and posited the *things-in-themselves* as unknown but existing realities. He comes very near to reality and then steps back, as if frightened by its stupendousness. The knowledge which one has of the Self cannot be the ground of the mill of the senses and reason, for, it is non-relative and constitutes an integral comprehension. It is beyond all conceivable proofs of knowledge, for it is the base of all proofs. To Kant, God is just an object of faith and not an object of experience. It is only when we narrow down the experience to the logical and empirical realms that we are inclined to dub it as a postulate.

The Dialectical Method of Hegel

Kant's critical method was taken much further up to its maximum limits and completed by Hegel in a staggering system of Idealism, built by means of what he termed as dialectical method. This method of Hegel consists in the constructive dialectical process of opposition and reconciliation. Thesis, anti-thesis and synthesis are its movements. The existence of the finite and its assertion of itself as such is the thesis. This thesis naturally evokes the existence and assertion of the finite that is its opposite, this is its anti-thesis. The relation between the thesis and the anti-thesis implies a reconciliation of these two in a higher synthesis brought about the evolving force of the whole, which transcends the isolated factors of the previous two. This results in the cooperation of both resulting in a blend of the existence and the assertion of the unity of the synthesis. Then this itself becomes a thesis to which rises an antithesis. The two again get unified and transcended in a still higher synthesis. This process gets transcended further into a still higher synthesis. This process continues in various grades progressively until the Absolute is reached, where all contradictions are finally and fully, reconciled. For Hegel, the form and matter of Kant constitute an organism in which they blend together to make up the universal whole. These forms are one with matter and thought is one with Reality while knowledge is Being itself. The internal and external are identical processes. The categories of Kant are the framework, not merely of thought, but of Reality itself.

According to Hegel, logic and metaphysics are one and the same. The study of reason is nothing but study of Reality while metaphysics is science of Reality. The real is the rational and the rational is the real. Hegel dismisses Kant's idea that the categories of knowledge are outside Reality and cannot be applied to the realm of Reality. In criticism of Kant he says—"thoughts do not stand between us and things, shutting us from things; they rather shut us together with them". He contends therefore that the categories of knowledge are present in the universal nature of Reality itself and are not confined merely to the knowing subject. The categories become the process of the development of thought through the dialectical movement of thesis, anti-thesis and synthesis, i.e., affirmation, opposition and reconcilation. Finally knowledge becomes identical with Reality, Being gets blended together with thought in the Absolute.

Here Hegel gives a concept of Reality. But he is not at all concerned with the possibility of experiencing it as one's Being itself. A careful critical study will show that even the dialectical method of Hegel does not give us knowledge of Pure Reality, but tries to only tabulate and examine the categories involved in one's attempt to group rationally the nature of Reality. Vedanta's, i.e. sanatana method's Absolutism is totally different from Hegel's, even though there are many resemblances between the two. Vedanta stands for pure non-sensory integral intuition and realisation in the form of experience, and not merely a rational concept like that of Hegel. Because in his method Hegel does not establish how thought and reality, logic and metaphysics are really one. It is with a lot of difficulty that one can prove the presence of the categories of knowledge in the frame-work of Reality. The dialectic way fails here. Surely Hegel, too, had a touch of some supernatural inspiration in him by which he posited the unity of Absolute, but not in its perfect sense. Because he was very much averse to anything that could not be subjected to the laws of reason. The Real is grasped only in Being and not by reason. That is where he fails.

The Analytical Method

The Socratic Analytical method of Philosophical disquisition is in arguing the entire anatomy of the subject in question, in the manner of a dialogue. The prima facie view is refuted by exposing the inconsistencies and contradictions involved in accepting it as true. The teacher pretends ignorance in the entire dialogue. Finally eliciting the truth from the mouth of the questioner himself; by ingenious method of subtle examination through questioning, dividing and analysis. This technique of argument is based on a complete knowledge of the fundamental component elements of the subject of argument and their relation to the constitution and condition of the intellect, as well as reason of the opposite party concerned in the discussion, and also in grounding the argument in the most basic facts acceptable to that party.

The Socratic method can be summed up as follows—*Firstly,* the assumption of an ignorance of Truth by the teacher, which is called as Socratic Irony. This attitude of intellectual humility and basing oneself on the most fundamental propositions in an agrument is essential to unravel the depth of Truth. Similarly was the case with Descartes, essential to unravel the depths of truth. *Secondly* the method of dialogue or conversation as an effective technique in the discovery of truth. This is based on a grasp of the presence of the knowledge of the true and the good in every person at the bottom of his Being, in spite of hasty decisions that one may take about things due to immature observations and prejudices. A common ground of truth among all can be brought out by careful analysis, argument and investigation through question and answer. This is called as art of philosophic midwifery. *Thirdly* the establishment of correct concepts or definitions before trying to know their application in life's particular instances. *Finally* the art of proceeding from the observed particular facts to more general truths. i.e., by adopting the inductive method of reasoning. Thus the analytical method of Socrates is also deductive in nature in the sense that it draws out the consequences and implications of certain concepts and tries to judge their validity.

The Synthetic Dialectic Method

This method was adopted by **Plato,** which concerned itself with discovering the causal relationship between thought and the Being. This method mostly consisted of the grouping of scattered particulars into a single concept or idea and again dissection of this concept or idea into classes, i.e., generalisation and arrangement of the ideas. The decisive form of fact depended on the establishment of a correct concept or notion or a principle. It is not possible to know the truth or goodness of anything, unless we first establish in our knowledge the nature of truth and goodness.

Pragmatic Method

The pragmatic method of **William James** accepts everything to be real when it tends to fruitful activity and results. The character of fulfilling the primal interests of man should be the guiding principle in Philosophy. Human interest is the touchstone of philosophical endeavour, of all activity-physical, mental, moral or spiritual. Values are to be judged by results, and the test of truth is its workability.

The **Psychological Method** of **Descartes** consisting of enquiring into the origin of ideas; **Bergson's Intuitional Method** in which biological evolution is the base; and finally **Spinoza's Geometrical method** are the techniques of much importance in getting towards the absolute truth.

The methods of **logical positivists, the naive realists,** and such others are not very relevant to endeavours directed towards arriving a consensus of Absolute Truth. Thus they may be discarded.

In the East mainly two methods are adopted—Purely intuitional and Realistic. Purely intuitional which is non-sensory and integral was the method of philosophy of the Vedas and the Upanishads, which is called as Sanātana method. Seers became one with Reality in intense concentration of mind, in meditation, in ecstasy, rapture and attunement ; then proclaimed to the world that the nature of Reality is non-duality, while the world seen is an illusory scenery on it. The Nyāya, Vāiśaiṣika, Sāṅkhya, Yoga and Mimāmsa philosophies propounded their experiences by a thoroughly realistic method of the analysis of experience. The Yoga system additionally pursued the psychological techniques of inner discipline while the Sanātana Method (Vedanta) followed a purely spiritual approach to life, backing it with a rigorous logical scrutiny and examination of experience. All these systems of the East have one common thing, i.e., Philosophy is an intensely practical affair, not just a theory. It is the art of wise way of living, the way of the attainment of salvation and freedom of the Empirical Self by the total experience of the pure non-dual Reality.

Nature of True Method of Philosophy

The method of philosophy in general is a comprehensive study of the totality of experience provided to us through all different sources of knowledge. In its vast studies, Philosophy takes into consideration the objects of the experience derived not only through the senses, understanding and reason, but also through mystical communion and realisation. While Science has no concern in the least-about such a study, because it has its special provinces of observation and experimentation only. Philosophy is a critical reflection on what is implied in experience, so that man can come in direct contact with it. All men do experience but all are not endowed with that higher faculty of reflecting upon what is lying deep in the experience. This higher reflection is the function of the Philosopher, and it is this that distinguishes him from the mass of mankind. The common man takes the world to be physical or phenomenal in its constitution, isolated by his own subjective self, and believes in the independent powers of the laws of nature over which he seems to have no control. Thus it is a superior understanding that discovers the supersensible fact of the organic-relation, which the outward universe has with man's essential intelligence. The truth is that man is not a puppet pulled by the strings held by an arbitrary nature. Life is not a mere puppet show, in which man is made to dance by strings pulled by a whimsical (unconstant and irregular) director. The universe is rather friendly and man is not only a organic part of it, but has in him the potentiality of knowing, ruling and coming into attunement with it. Philosophy, therefore, corrects the commonsense notions of the unreflective mind, and thus becomes a great universal remedy for all ill of life caused by ignorance and impotency of one's Self.

The validity of genuine philosophical truths lies in their universality, practicality and necessity. Thus they are not in need of any further verification of their tenabilility. As they are illuminated by the torch of intuition, any external verification of their validity is not only not necessary but meaningless too. They are always characterised by immediacy, universality and necessity and, consequently, by infallibility and perfect veracity. They hold good for all minds in all conditions, for they spring from the depths of knowledge. There are certain features of reality pervading every ordinary experience, recognisable through subtle contemplation and reflection. The very purpose of Philosophy is to study these all pervasive features of reality making themselves felt in experience, so that by means of these visible subtle features man may be in a position to rise directly to an intuition of what they feebly indicate.

It is a very big foolish mistake made by many thinkers (Eastern or Western) to reject all super-rational experience as irrational and debar it from the field of Philosophical studies. Facts that reason cannot know, are not therefore infra-rational. When it becomes impossible for reason to comprehend certain truths, it is not fair to reject them as anti-rational. We cannot subject super sensible facts to the categories of our knowledge, but they can be logically deduced from such facts, without our being irrational.

Q: What a common student of Philosophy actually means when he says that super-sensory realities are irrational?

Ans: They are totally dissimilar to all phenomona that are known to him by the senses. Actually dissimilarity to rational concepts is not always irrationality. What is beyond reason is known in a knowledge which is private from the point of view of the person who has it, but is universal in itself. The impossibility of communicating such knowledge through the usual visible means of the world has led many to the false notion that it does not exist at all. Concepts evolved from sense-experience are powerless in judging the nature of the ultimate cause of all causes- The indubitable non-dual Self. No one can deny one's own Self or his being conscious of his Self, or can deny his consciousness which is beyond the senses and reason. Thus it is necessary to try to get a deep insight of the Sanatana method of philosophy, which is being done in the next chapter.

5

The Sanātana Method

The Sanatana method combines revelation, meditation and reason in one. This has been adopted by the Vedantins of the East. All methods of sense-function and mental approach to Truth have to be set aside as faulty for the reason that their deliverances are untrustworthy, being logically indefensible and psychologically worked by the defects of the instruments. Infallible knowledge can be had only by nonsensory intuition of the Reality because knowledge attained by senses, understanding and reason falls short of it in an enormous degree. No other method than direct communion with Being as such confine us ultimate reliable knowledge of the Truth, pure reality. Untill the knower and the known are identically separate in knowledge, knowledge is not true, but it can give us only a semblance of what we seek to obtain.

The experience of the nature of the individual in relation to the universe, of which it is a content, becomes the basics of philosophical enquiry, which culminates in spiritual meditation and Realization. Authority (Vedas), Reason (Yukti) and intuition (Sakshat Anubhava)—are the stages of the ascent of the Soul aspiring for eternal life. Study (Sravana), Reflection (Manana) and Meditation (Nididhyasana) - sum up the practical method of the spiritual aspirant. Study and Reflection comprise the entire gamut of speculative Philosophy while Meditation is the final fruitition leading to Realization (Sakshatkara). Aspiration for the eternal is the basic and the greatest incentive to philosophical enquiry, whose aim is not only to *know*, but to *be*.

Human knowledge is neither exact representation of Reality, nor is the world a mere projection of mind. The world is an objective appearance of the absolute, thus being ideal, but is also the cause of the representation of the same in human knowledge, thus being real. Therefore the world is ideal as knowledge, thus being real. Therefore the world is ideal as contained in the Absolute, real as being outside the finite minds in the empirical and apparent views and totally unreal (illusory) as truth in the view of the Absolute. The variety observed in sensations should prove that there is variety in objects which are not sensation in themselves. Philosophical techniques rise from the establishment of Self as the source of knowledge. Therefore, philosophy should proceed with equipments that bear relations to the Self primarily, for, bereft of knowledge of this unavoidable relation, any enterprise in this direction is bound to be energy wasted like a wild goose chase. There is a fundamental co-relativity of all things as values emerging from and converging in the Self, which is unmistakably the unchanging centre of all experience. The question of the existence and the nature of this Self will be discussed properly in its proper place. How are we to be sure that the method which we employ to achieve a certain end is valid or not? Perhaps, in ordinary life, this will be accepted for by the possibility at least of a hope for accomplishing the purpose in view. But even for that we will have to sift well the material that we have in our hands and judge the strength and usefulness of it before we actually use or proclaim. A thorough knowledge of the correctness and the satisfactory character of the method has always to precede the employment of the same for the chosen purpose. We should not make assertions or take hasty active steps without first ascertaining the powers of the instruments of knowledge and action. **Sir Prichard** has rightly stated in his work "Kant's theory of knowledge" that—"we must understand what knowing is, in order to explain anything at all, so that-any proposed explanation of knowing would necessarily presuppose that we understood—'what knowing is'."

The Absolute, i.e., Atman which is pure reality, which cannot be gainsaid and which is the presupposition of experience, is the pivot of all Philosophical disquisitions.

The central aim of the true Philosophy is the living of the highest life, a life fixed in the knowledge of the principle the soul which is the ultimate generator, regulator and destroyer of all things. An enlightened light of peace and joy is the goal of a sublime Philosophy. And this blessedness can be attained only in the Divine Being. The Ethical value (Dharma), the Material value (Artha) and the Vital value (Kama) are all based on Liberation (Moksha) which is the supreme value of existence. Thus the aim of life is to attain liberation, i.e., Total freedom and everlasting absolute bliss.

The sight of evil and suffering, pain and death, etc... directs one's vision to the causes of this dualistic phenomenon; and this, necessiates an enquiry into the reality behind life as a whole. Thus it is not just an academic interest in theoretical pursuits, but a practical irresistible urge to experience reality, that leads to the glorious enterprise of a True Philosophy.

In the East, Philosophy does not pretend to provide any new knowledge which was not existent before but elaborately expounds the structure of the eternal knowledge which is being handed by the ancient Sages through several generations. Thus there is no one single Philosopher but there are links in the long chain of seers who have imparted their spiritual wisdom to mankind through precept as well as by practice. The core of a True-Philosophy stresses on the need of intense meditations that lead a seeker to an ineffable spiritual experience, which is neither sensory nor intellectual but timeless, spaceless and objectless.

The True Philosophy teaches that the bondage of man is due to his ignorance of true nature of his ownself and therefore his freedom is in the right knowledge of Self. Bondage means subjection to the process of birth and death leading to the consequent experience of suffering and pain. Self knowledge has to be attained in this very life by putting forth sufficient effort towards this end. True absolute happiness can be had only in the Self. Thus it is futile to search for it in this illusory temporal world, which does not partake of the nature of reality. The Knowledge for which Man has to strive for is just not a theoretical understanding but is the consciousness of the Self itself. It is neither information gathered regarding the Self nor a mere acquaintance with it through discursive reason, that can liberate man from his bondage. What is required is practical realization, which is possible only through profound meditation on the nature of Self. This type of meditation is again impossible without strict self-discipline and self-restraint. As Self is the true pure reality, the means of its realisation should also be necessarily totally pure. That means a conscious abandonment of desires for objects that exist as non-self and that create an apparent division between consciousness and its natural contents. This Philosophy is the living of a life full of deep insight and an intense austerity consequent upon it, whose final aim is to assure the experience of total absolute bliss of Self in one's own Self. Once having attained it the life of the realized will be to render help to rest of humanity for reaching this glorious consummation of life by teaching and personal example or may lead a totally renunciate life as per the body's fate. It is not a study confined to schools but is a study of the technique of wise living by grounding oneself in the consciousness of the Self and living with wisdom. In other words it is learning to manifest the law of the Eternal in the temporal life of the world, to bring a reconciliation between the absolute and the relative. Philosophy is the life of a true human being unceasingly alive to and in the presence of the supermundane Absolute.

True Philosophy is not any secret tenet to be tread on by a select few, i.e., it is beyond caste, creed, religion, country and other bondages and limitations. It is an all-inclusive method which comprises all existent means of communion with Reality. It is really the Vedanta applied to all aspects of life in order to live one's life at its highest and best. It is the system of perfect life, the rule of wisdom and the law of liberty. That is why it is called as "Sanātana Dharma", an ever lasting all-pervasive law of life. Therefore, it is not a speculative system reserved for intellectual pleasantry during leisure hours, but is the food of higher understanding and the light of the True Self of man.

Every citizen of the world can be taught this universal Philosophy. Thus this should be the basic Human Right, as it is the goal of life. But the teacher should know well what it truly means and how it can be applied in practice to the different stages of life and to different individuals. It is due to ignorance and wrong understanding or prejudice that make certain people think that this Sanatana method is an other worldly theory concerning only a life which is possible after death. This is a totally false perception as the Sanatana Method of Philosophy is not any narrow dogma divorced from the facts of everyday life but is the only true and best way of living a life, as it can be and ought to be applied in the daily life of everyone. Without it life would be a perpetual groping in darkness. What is man? He is not a thought or a feeling or a group of thoughts and feelings. Man is truly the Absolute Pure Reality itself, which is self-luminous, illumining the world of thought, of feeling, of understanding, of willing and of reason. It is the life of the thoughtful, the joy of the learned, the destination of the pilgrim soul on the arduous path of knowledge. It is the final explanation of the Yoga of action, devotion, concentration, wisdom and of every conceivable religious, philosophic or mystic methodology.

The Vedanta, i.e., The Sanatana's integral method, which has all the characteristics of a True Philosophy, does not teach that one should detest the world or isolate oneself in some world other than this. It does not proclaim that anyone should forsake his duties in life or put on a grave face or behave in any conspicious manner. Vedanta declares that one should not be selfish or attached to any fleeting object, one should live in the consciousness of the loving brotherhood and unity of the self in the universe. It states clearly that the truth of existence is one and indivisible therefore division or separation, hatred and enemity, quarrel and selfishness etc... are against the nature of one's Self. It declares that the pain of birth and death is due to desires generated by the ignorance of one's Self, which is the root cause of all miseries. It propounds that the highest state of experience is immortal life or the realization of the Self. Birth is for this supreme purpose and thus this is the highest duty of man, while all other duties are only aids or auxilliary to this paramount duty. To attain liberation one has to perform one's prescribed duties with the spirit of non-attachment and dedication of one's self and one's actions to the supreme being. It finally sums up stating that every aspect of one's life should get consummated in this consciousness.

Therefore the question is not of abandoning something or holding on to something, but of a change in the vision of life. It is a reorientation in the way of the functioning of the volitional, the conceptual and the perceptual consciousness that is required for the Philosophic life. Because the body will be there; the activities will be there; but these have to be transformed only into the lustrousness of the liberated life by the touch of the

Philosopher's stone of the knowledge of Self. This life of Self knowledge is the goal of True Philosophy, by which life is in its splendid perfection and plentitude. This is the blessed state of complete freedom. The way to such realization is the Sanātana Integral Intuition method, called as Vedanta. To attain the goal one has to know the target. Here the target is Self perception. Therefore one has to attain the knowledge of the nature of Self perception, for which one has to have an analytical knowledge of Self. Thus, in next chapter, let us briefly discuss on the analysis of Self.

6

An Analysis of Self

The Knower or the Self cannot be a thing, subject to development or process of evolution, as some thinkers opine. Because development would mean the cessation of the Self at some particular instant of time. Change means the ending of one condition and the beginning of another different from the previous one. If the Self is to undergo change, it has to modify its essence in the course of time, then there would be nothing as a permanently enduring subject of knowledge. Thus the essence of the Self can either be of changable or developable nature. This is very clear by the fact that even change or development could not be known without the assumption of a synthesising consciousness behind the process and the chain of change or development. Therefore the Self is to be accepted as a changeless, permanent and an ever enduring Being. That means naturally, the Self is totally different from process or development or evolution. The Self is non-temporal, is not involved in the time process; for time is an object of its knowledge. Now let us briefly go through both Western and Sanatana views regarding self.

The Nature of Self

The Western Views:

1. The view of **Prof. Taylor** that the Self has for its exclusive material our emotional interests and purposive attitudes towards the various constitutents of our surroundings, cannot be accepted for the reason that no process of any kind can be admitted into the Self. A purposive attitude is a psychical condition, always changing, and so dying on to itself and thus is not identical with the Self in any way. Even the continuity of a pervading purpose has to become the object of consciousness, for, otherwise, such a purpose cannot exist as a reality. We know of no reality which is unrelated to consciousness in some way or the other. There cannot be a process without something in which

it appears of which it is a temporal condition. A purpose or interest is a temporal flow which ought to become an object of Knowledge. A sustained purpose or an interest is only the maintenance of a continuous psychic function animated by an underlying consciousness which is totally different from it. The Self is therefore, a transcendent consciousness bringing order to all relational phenomenon, but itself remaining beyond all relations.

2. The view of **Leibnitz** and others that the Self is a monad, spiritual in nature but different from other monads governing the psycho-physical organism, does not stand scrutiny; so also the theory of many selves. If the Self is a unit centralised among diverse psychic contents or the parts that constitute the body, its relation to the latter becomes unintelligible. Is the spiritual monad identical with the contents of the organism or different from them? If it is different from the organismic contents then it cannot be called the Self of man because it would remain unrelated to the other parts which are equally essential for the personality of man. Moreover, the Self could not know that it has an individual organ, for it would lie outside the knowledge of the Monad. If the Monad has a relation to the psychical and physical contents then it would cease to be a simple monad, self existing and unrelated. So what we should accept is that the Self pervades the entire organism and that the latter has no existence independent of the former.

3. The view that senses are themselves Self as accepted by some **materialists** cannot be accepted as they are not conscious by themselves, for they are instruments of knowledge. The senses are objective. They only bring about a relation between the subject and the object. An instrument is always used by another which is different from it. The functions of the senses are diverse, therefore each cannot be a Self. If any one of the senses is accepted as Self, then in the view of the other senses it is not acceptable; as there will be quarrel and disharmony. To synthesise the sensations into percepts and concepts an intelligent principle different from them will have to be accepted. If all the senses are to be regarded as the Self, then there would be many Selves in each body leading to no knowledge of any kind. Because plurality cannot be explained without a basal unity. Even when there are no objects and the senses are suspended,

there remains the consciouness of one's being felt as in deep sleep. Hence consciousness is not the senses. The Self can never be diversified and changeful like the senses.

4. Consciousness cannot be the body or a property of the body itself as perviewed by **Hume** and some materialists, for, the latter is its object. Self cannot be subservient to its own object. The body never becomes the knower, it always remains the known. If consciousness were the essence of the body, then, as the essence of a thing cannot ever cease to be, there would be no death of the body or its bereavement from consciousness. It is seen that the body is used as an instrument of action by all internal conscious functions which are illuminated by the Self. If the body or the essence of the body would be consciousness then there would not be a disintegration of the parts of the body, as for Self is indivisible. If it is divisible, then one division would be an object of the other division. But no one experiences so. The body is inert and perishable and thus consciousness in it has come through mind and senses.

5. According to some Philosopher's view the activity in general is itself Self. The Truth is that Self has no relation to activity, for the latter is an external relation, and so non-eternal, while the Self is eternal. There cannot be any action without a spatial and temporal existence of its subject to any modification. Action can abide in an individual but not in the Self. There cannot be action without duality, whereas Self in its true sense is non-dual. Action is an indication of imperfection an effort to overcome an existing defect, while Self is nothing else than total perfection. Self is totally different from internal activities too, such as desire, volition, etc., for they are as external and as much in need of the phenomenon of duality as the physical actions.

6. Self, i.e., Consciousness is not a mere property, a quality or an attribute of something eternal as per some other's view. If Consciousness is a quality of the Self then what is the essential nature of the Self? It should be different from Consciousness, i.e., an unconscious entity. On such a supposition we will not be able to account for the subject nature of consciousness and object-nature of the rest of the world. Because an attribute or quality or property cannot be identical with the substance in which it inheres. Therefore we will have to say that the self is an object of the consciousness. But it is absurd to think so. All attempts

to give the Self i.e., pure consciousness itself by essence, a tinge of objectivity ends in failure. Because it is impossible to establish any difference between Self and Consciousness.

7. Psycho-analysis considers consciousness as only a partial censored expression of the vast reservoir of the unconscious which is the ultimate cause of all individual functions and activities. This view of **James, Schopenhauer, Neitzsche**, **Freud** and all others who are under the influence of Modern Psychology does not stand scrutiny. They say that Intellectual activity is said to be an expression of hidden unconscious impulses. Consciousness and Reason, both are subordinated to unconscious urges, cravings, appetites etc...; all of which are expressions of man's natural biolcgical interests like sex, hunger, self-preservation, love for power, etc... The essence of the consciousness is thus traced back to unconscious. The difficulty here is that the existence of the unconscious is discovered only by the operations of the consciousness. This is called as mutual dependence, which is an abrogate in testimony of Philosophy. Unconscious cause cannot bring out a conscious effect, as cause and effect are mutually related and what is not in the cause cannot be present in the effect. If conciousness were an effect then it would be an object external, but we exprience it always to be the knowing subject of all else. Even the unconsciousness is an object of the consciousness. It may be considered the individual empirical consciousness and reason exhibit elements drawn from an unconscious matrix of instinctive urges; but the innermost universal pure consciousness that is behind this instinctive to non-instinctive urges and all else, when rationalised is found to be not the same as the unconscious. Some add sub-conscious too inbetween, but by the abovesaid argument even that does not stand scrutiny. Thus consciousness is not an outcome of the unconscious.

8. Some Philosophers (Behaviourists) have postulated that consciousness is the result of aggregates of Physical and Physiological motions or external behaviour. This again is a tantamount to the materialist theory that the Self can be a product or mixture of the unconscious elements. Behaviour, which is observed in bodies moved by the nervous system cannot be supposed to be the source of consciousness. Because behaviour is a function of the psycho-physical organism and merely of the

body. Behaviour is external, whereas Self is eternal which is the observer of the behaviour, thus Self cannot be the product of Behaviour. On the other hand Behaviour is the object of the subject Self. Behaviour is the visible physical manifestation of the manner in which the internal psyche works through the instrumentality of the body and the nervous system. This controlling system is as much physical as the outer body, and so it cannot be the source of knowledge, i.e., Pure Consciousness i.e., Self. Also it is consciousness that is pre-supported even in the observation of the behaviour. The behaviourists think that sensations, perceptions, thoughts, emotions and the like are reducible to physical or physiological reflexes. But they forget that the physical and the physiological phenomenon are external and are dependent of consciousness for their happening or existence. Thus they cannot be identified with it or considered to be its origin.

9. Attempts were also made to reduce the Self to a kind of expression of some neutral stuff existing as its raw-material by **Russell** and others. Even **William James** states that experience is a relation which has subject and object in it. Knower and known are divisions within a pri-mordial experience. Thus he says- "There is only one primal stuff or material in the world, of which everything is composed, and if we call that stuff as–'Pure experience', then knowing can easily be explained as a particular relation of one another. The relation itself is a part of pure experience, into which all other portions (elements) of pure exprience enter. Mind and matter are constructed out of natural neutral stuffs and entities." This cannot be true because that neutral stuff has to be either consciousness or un-consciousness. If it is thė former, then, there cannot be many other consciousnesses proceeding from it, as there cannot be two consciousnesses relating to each other as cause and effect. If it is the latter, then, production of concsiousness from un-consciousness becomes unintelligible. Because what is present in the effect should be in the cause. Then either the pure experience of James should be identical to consciousness or it should be the primordial condition of the manifestation of an empirical consciousness, which is the effect of an universal cause, the Absolute, the Self, Pure Reality.

10. The self cannot be identified with the principle of life or *elanvital,* i.e. the life principle, considered as supreme in experience, of which matter and consciousness are only expressions or subsidiaries; as done by **Bergson**. He states that matter is a self-created obstruction onto the march of the *elanvital* and consciousness is also a self-created light for illuminating the path of its evolution. Even this view is false. As the life principle-*elanvital* can be known to exist only on the assumption of a conscionsness, which is Absolute existence-bliss-knowledge. If consciousness is a product then it is subject to destruction and it cannot be reality underlying the life-process. Also, matter cannot be an auxiliary to consciousness, for it is an object of consciousness, the life principle is just a bond between the body and the mind. Life is above matter but below mind, intellect and consciousness. Matter, life, mind, intellect and senses are all empirical categories and thus they cannot be the universal absolute consiousness.

11. The Realist's and the non-Hegelian's view is that the mind and its objects (matter) are on a par with each other, differing only in their properties and functions. The biggest mistake committed here is that a unifying Self above the mind and its objects is not detected and accepted. As one cannot say that cognition is a mere relation and that the mind with its objects are known to be related to one another in a *compresence,* in which the related terms stand to each other having the same reality. But this is possible only if there is a Self which knows them both in a single act of perception. Neither the mind nor the objects can be known to exist if they are entirely different from one another. Thus a knowledge of two different entities implies a permanent consciousness holding them without which not only this relation but even their existence cannot be proved. While the existence of a permanent Self as the pure-consciousness beyond mind and objects remains self-proved by the fact that without it none of our experiences can be satisfactorily accounted for. If knowledge is a relation by *compresence,* then it cannot know the terms related, unless it transcends them. Therefore an absolute spiritual being, which transcends all in knowing and being is self-proved.

12. The view of some other philosophers' is that every passing thought can be considered as the true subject of

knowledge cannot be accepted. If any particular knowledge is to be considered as the ultimate knowing subject, then it would be unrelated to the other thoughts that occur in the mind. Further, it would be impossible on this hypothesis to account for memory of the past or anticipation of the future. Thus the self is totally different from the assemblege of the psychical functions and conditions which contribute to the manifestation of knowledge. It cannot be a product of any collection of circumstances externally related to one another. It is not also a totality of situations or a series of appearances or of the nature of duality itself without a unifying subject independent of its terms.

13. The Self cannot be accepted to be a stream of consciousness as propogated by **Buddhists** and some westerners. Because a stream is a movement and a movement cannot know itself, as its very essence is change. We do not have any experience of such a flow or stream which has no bed on which it flows. Thus one will have to assume a permanent non-changing absolute consciousness on which this empirical stream of consciousness is flowing. Therefore the Self cannot be any kind of process for every process is an object of knowledge. Any part or item of process cannot itself be aware of the entire process. A process has a meaning only when it is known by a Being which is not involved in the process, but is the witness of the process. The Self is of such a nature that it is not analysable into constituents, for anything that is subject to division or change is temporal and perishable.

14. As some assume the Self to be momentary is also a fallacy, for the above said reasons and that which is momentary is always destructible and cannot be the subject of knowledge. The perception of momentariness is due to a succession of the appearance of objects at different instants of time. It is not the self that is momentary, but the perception of objects determined by the nature of the appearence of objects to consciousness. Momentary elements are those which are known by consciousness but not the knower itself. Because the proofs by which the objects are known are based on the self-evident, self-luminous and pure conscious nature of the Self.

15. Descartes, Whitehead and some others view is that the Self is one with the object which it knows and is on the same level of reality with them, forming an organism or an organ. If it were so, there would be darkness enveloping all things, for want of a knowing Self. The objects can never determine the Self, for it is beyond them in every way. It is not of the nature of difference—in fact it has no relation to difference – and the differences that are observed in the forms of knowledge are due to the differences in structure and conditions of the objects presented to the consciousness, but not of consciousness itself. Consciousness does not create the object but just reveals them in perception. They appear to be related to Self due to mental modification. It is due to delusion that one is not able to identify separately the Self and the object even though they are of totally opposite nature. The objects are not even the modes in the perceiving consciousness, they are different from it, though the essence of both is the Absolute. Because it is the absolute that integrates all sensations and perceptions into a coherent whole.

16. **Aristotle** and some others view is that Self is a phenomenon; even this does not stand scrutiny. If consciousness were a changing phenomenon then a synthesis of knowledge would be impossible and there would arise a contingency of introducing different consciousnesses at different times. In order to justify such consciousnesses, they have to be known by another consciousness, which we have to admit to be the real Self. That real Self should be one, and not more than one, for no one ever feels that one is also divisible. Everyone knows that one's Self cannot be cut or divided into segments. Even to suppose that the Self can be manifold would lead to the necessity of a unifying unitary consciousness which will know the difference between the segments assumed in the Self. If the Self were not self-luminous, self-evident and non-dual then when it manifests objects there would be a doubt as to whether the cognition is there or not, whether the objects exist or not. But no one experiences such a doubt at the time of cognition. Thus memory, cognition, existence of objects, duality and phenomenon establish the self identity of knowledge, i.e., Self-potent Self. Because the passing forms of perception are not the Self, for they require another Self known by their mutual relation.

17. The view of **Immanuel Kant** is that the Self is an object of reason though it is not an object of any sense, is also false. Here, object of reason means, a thing only knowable by

Reason and never be experienced but would just be a matter of faith. If it could be an object then one would feel the 'I' at the time of a particular condition of a 'this' or a 'that' and none would experience an 'I-consciousness'. Moreover, the Self, while becoming an object would also become inert and a transient material entity like the other objects of the world. To justify the very admission of a world-process a self-proved independent consciousness has to be assumed. Kant himself while repudiating Hume's view has indirectly accepted a self-evident self-luminous Self. Because according to **Hume** impressions and ideas are related to one another by the laws of association, on this Kant urges that the fact of the association of ideas points to a deeper unifying function of Self, which he terms "the transcendental unity of apperception": Even this conclusion of Kant is based on reason only. For, he never accepts a non-mediate intuition to experience it. But according to the Sanatana's True Philosophy only this transcendental Self should not be supposed to be totally abstracted from the empirical Self. As the former is immanent in the appearance of the latter. The aim of support to an empirical Self is self-transcendence. **Mackenzie** has put this Sanatana view in almost perfect words in his work—*Manual of Ethics* (p. 274) "In order to do this (true transcendence to experience pure reality), we must negate the merely individual (empirical) Self, which is not the True Self. We must realise ourselves by sacrificing ourselves. The more fully we so realise ourselves, the more do we reach a universal point of view, i.e., a point of view from which our own private good is no more to us than the good of anyone else". **Green** also similarly observes that the relation of events to each other as in time implies their equal presence to a subject which is beyond time and space. There could be no such object as time, if there is no self-consciousness which is not in time. Even though both Mackenzie and Green accept a self-evident universal consciousness as Self, pervading space and time but still they are short of the pure reality because Self is not only beyond space and time but beyond universal good too, for everything that we perceive is the effect of delusion, i.e., Illusion.

18. Even **Bradley** who is very close to Sanatana's True Philosophy also has done a mistake by supposing the Self and its objects to be interchangeable. He states that any particular

appearance of the Absolute can be either a subject or an object-according to the standpoint from which we judge a particular appearance and the emphasis on which we lay by making it the exclusive subject of our consideration. As already discussed by many arguments it does not require much intelligence to understand that the True Self can never become an object, for the object is always insentient in nature while the Self is always sentient. The two are opposed to each other in their constitution and mode of operation in the process of perception. The ordered nature of the world owes its existence to an indivisible unchangeable Self which is its knower. The Self is therefore not an empirical subject, as it is beyond the space-time manifold. Even space-time [Alexander's view], substance [Spinoza], rational intellect [Hegel] are those which are presented as an object to a knower subject. That Knower, Self, cannot be grasped by knowledge through the categories in terms of which the senses and mind operate within the realms of matter. Therefore the existence of the Self is established negatively by the predicates of experience and positively by the self-evident consciousness which one has of oneself at all times. The subject, object and their relation are to be comprehended in a universal Self. Thus the True Self of man is not an empirical bundle of psychic contents, which is interchangeable with other such congeries and by mistake, this empirical confuses with the real Self.

By the above discursive brief discussion of the different views of the Western Philosophers, it is clear that none of them could reach or had experienced the True Self. Now to get a clear picture of the nature of the True self it is necessary to summarise the Sanatana Philosophy and try to realise the True Self and its nature.

The Nature of True Self : (Sanatana View)

The existence of an immutable consciousness is self evident from the implications of our experience in the three phenomenal states-waking, dreaming and deep sleep. Even though it is self-evident but either due to self-ignorance and illusion or due to super-imposition or duality by the primordial matter called "Maya", everybody, including great thinkers, are not able to experience it.

In the waking state, the individual identifies itself with the physical body and feels his essence and existence to be identical with the visible gross vesture. But this assertion of the oneness of one's essence and existences with the physical body is contradicted and disproved in dream. Because the individual in dream exists with various kinds of experience. But this external physical body then is disconnected from consciousness. Therefore a dreaming person does not have any exterior physical experience which implies that senses of waking state are not the external organs of sense but certain internal force is the avenue of a perception during waking state. It is that internal force which disassociates itself from the physical body when one is in the state of dream.

Now, Is the dreaming person, who is disassociated from his physical body in the dreaming state, the real person identical with this body or not? Here we are forced to believe that we are not the physical body. Otherwise we should have experienced it even in dream. Similarly, neither even the dreaming person, dream body nor the objects, etc..., therein can be identified with the highest consciousness. As in deep sleep, even the dreaming person with all his accessories is separated from experience and there it appears to be nothing at all. The person seems to be bereft of the value and content of all conscious experience. Everything that is known in the state of waking and dreaming are cast aside and the personality withdraws itself from all objective conditions. What, then, is the nature of the person who is the experiencer of things in all the states with its contents. We have, perforce, to admit, that what is experienced in deep sleep is ultimate reality. But, Is this position correct? Are we conscious in that state? The answer is, no. Are we then, in ignorant state essentially? No one would agree to this position too. Thus to decide we have to think over the expression of the memory of the deep sleep experience which one express when one wakes up from deep sleep. I had a happy-relaxed-sound sleep and I didn't experience anything—This is what we remember about deep sleep which reflects the contents of deep sleep, which states that there was ignorance and bliss, i.e., the experience of ignorance and bliss. In other words, we had conscious experience in deep sleep, whose object was ignorance. Thus the nature of consciousness that existed in deep sleep was conscious experience.

From the nature of the deep sleep experience the argument put forth is that consciousness has been covered by some obstructing factor (ignorance) in deep sleep. But consciousness as such was never non-existent. If it had been non-existent then we could not have a memory of having slept soundly. Therefore we have to admit that consciousness is the only ever existing continuous essential element in our life - waking, dream and deep sleep states. It persists in all states of experience, even in swoon or death. Behind every thought, thought of existence or non-existence, there is consciousness. Something self-luminous always exists and persists. Even the Nihilist, who denies everything, exists. Denial is preceded by the consciousness of denial. This consciousness subtratum is ultimate Reality. It is Pure Self. Thus the essence of the personality and individuality of man is this pure consciousness. This is true existence. It is the only existence also, for it is the sole unchanging Being which survives during all change, surpasses all that we know and while everything that we consider as our own desert us, it never deserts us. This alone can be eternal.

It is what is in the past, present and future alike; without a beginning, middle or end; unchanging its nature-consciousness-existence-bliss; not conditioned by space, time and causation; which endures waking, dream and deep sleep; which is of the nature of one homogeneous essence. Such an existence is not an attribute of the Self, but is its essence. Self is not existent but existence itself. It is our experience, rather an inherent feeling, that we never were not, and that we never shall cease to be, though our physical bodies may disappear. This is a reflection of the permanent existence of an eternal pure true Self within us. We all know that we are here in this world, that we exist, and this experience asserts itself independent of all mental endeavour. In order to experience the fruitition of actions which appear in the form of a continuous change, the same Self has to be admitted to exist in the infinite past, similarly in the infinite future too. The pure Self ought to exist as the underlying consciousness of the empirical Self, equally in the past, present and future. Without the pure self as base the outward phenomena of the world can have no existence of their own. Thus pure Self is the absolute Existence and the only pure Reality.

It is a self-luminous absolute consciousness. It shines by itself unaided by any other light, it illumines the whole world by its light. One may ask—how can we illumine the world when we are ignorant and dependant on external light to perceive the world. The answer is as follows—The universe that we know, is of two kinds—the external and the internal. The external world consists of the five elements—ether, air, fire, water and earth with their properties sound, touch, form, taste and smell. The combinations of these elements resulting into the gross world, full of different names and forms possessing infinite qualities and shapes. The external universe is always an object of consciousness and is experienced to be inert. It is we that know the universe, the universe does not know us. That means external universe becomes an object of our Self when a flood of light of our consciousness is thrown upon it. The internal universe consists of the five sheaths, viz., the physical, vital, mental, intellectual and blissful; the three bodies, viz., the gross, subtle and the causal; the six changes, viz., relativity of existence, birth, growth, change, decay and destruction; and the six waves, viz., birth and death, hunger and thirst, grief and delusion. This entire inner world, also, is inert; for it exhibits such a nature in dreamless sleep state. At that time it is only the Self that shines independently without any external phenomena. So it is clear here that it is by the light of the self-luminous absolute consciousness that everything shines but appears to be possessed by the intelligence. When knowledge of the Self dispels the ignorance, the Self shines in its native glory and unsurpassed splendour just like gold, which shines when fire dispels the dross. The dispelling power is also borrowed by the knowledge from the Self itself. Therefore the Upanishad declares "There the sun does not shine, nor the moon, nor the stars; there these lightnings do not shine; what to say about this fire". "Everything shines after Him that shines; all this is illuminated by His light".

The nature of Self is absolute bliss. The pleasure that we derive from objects, such as building, rooms, comfortable furnitures, women, etc..., is temporary and subject to the limiting adjunct or vehicle of the five sheaths and it has degrees too. The greatest happiness that man knows is in the state of deep sleep. Because here the happiness is not caused by any external object, but is the spontaneous manifestation of the Self with a veil of ignorance. Hence the happiness of deep sleep is far superior to all other forms of happiness experienced either in waking or dream state. It is not mere absence of pain but positive peace independent of all external causes. It is this happiness that everyone eagerly longs for and prepares soft beds, pillows, etc. to induce the mind to go to sleep simultaneously one even dislikes all those causes which may be hindrances on the way of one's enjoying such happiness. Without the veil of ignorance the absolute bliss of pure Self has no degrees, while the relative happiness beginning from the state of micro-organisms insects etc... upto attributive God (Saguṇa Brahman-Ishwara or Hiranyagarbha) has degrees with admitted differences.

One may argue that the bliss of dreamless sleep cannot be eternal, as if it would be eternal than we should experience it in all the states. But this is not so, for the bliss of the Pure Self which is fully manifest in dreamless sleep partially expresses itself through the psychoses (vritti) of the mind in waking and dream states also. But the spiritual bliss is not fully manifest in waking or dream state, because it is restricted by the mental and sensual processes. Though the sense-pleasures caused by object of fulfilled desires seem to veil the bliss of Pure Self, but actually they owe their origin to the Self. Thus the absolute bliss is unobstructed at all times, but it is not always known to be such on account of the mental and sensual modifications. The happiness born of mental or sensual contact with objects is known empirically, for here happiness is objectified. But the bliss of the Self is not thus known, for, when one experiences the Self one becomes the embodiment of bliss. Therefore it is said to be Absolute.

It is the ego in the waking and dream states and ignorance in sleep that veil the Self and do not let one experience the pure Self as absolute bliss. Even though the bliss of the infinite is the real object of pure love, but the infinite is objectified, and it is the concentration of the mind on objectness that is the hideous error in all forms of love. True pure love lets one experience the supreme bliss which is sought wrongly in objects appearing limited by space and time. Therefore Upanishads declare—The

Self is dearer than wife, dearer than children, dearer than nation, king, religion, religious texts, money and all else. Everything is dear and loveable on account of the love of the Self, i.e., of supreme absolute bliss. This shows that one's greatest desire is to overcome all pains and enjoy everlasting freedomful bliss. As the Self alone is indestructible, such bliss rests in Self alone.

The Absolute Existence-Consciousness-Bliss is realized to be the essential nature of Pure Self. These properties are not three different elements constituting the Self. And also these are not its attributes or qualities. They form one indivisible whole soul. Existence is itself Consciousness and Bliss also. Similarly Consciousness is itself Existence and Bliss. Bliss too itself is the Existence and Consciousness. There cannot be any kind of limitation or division in the absolute Pure Self. Limitation conceived is of three kinds: Limitation by space, by time and by individuality. But space, being an effect, cannot condition the Self which is the ultimate cause of all causes. Space has a beginning and an end, it originates at the time of creation and is transcended in self-realization, and so it is not eternal. All, that is not eternal is different from the Self and has no relation to it. Self is also not limited by time, for the time is a process, which is nothing but a consciousness of succession of spatial events arisen in the temporal perception of the sense organs. As the Self is unconditioned by the mental processes, it is beyond time. All that are conditioned by time are seen to be perishable, and so the Self which is eternal is ought to transcend time. The Self is not limited by individualities or objects that fill the world and form its constituents. Limitation by object is also of three kinds: by the existence of a similar object, a dissimilar object and due to internal variety or differentiation within oneself. For example, existence of a mango tree is limited by the existence of another mango tree, by the existence of rocks, and by trunk, branches, leaves, flowers, fruits, etc in it. The Self is free from internal variety and external differentiation, for anything that have these limitations has to be within the limits of space and time, and so perishable. The eternal Self is untouched by the three kinds of limitations which characterises the objects of the world only.

This concept of Self, to be of the nature of pure Absolute Existence-Consciousness-Bliss is only provisional and negative definition provided as an intellectual prop for understanding and meditation. The true Pure Self is, in fact, beyond even this concept. As this concept is postulated keeping in view this empirical world. The world is found to be lacking the character of Pure Absolute Existence, i.e., Reality. Because the world is unreal, and so, in contradistinction from it, the Self is said to be Pure Absolute Existence and Reality. The world is experienced to be of the nature of being inert, objective and changing; and so, the Self which is different from the world is declared to be self-luminous Consciousness. The world is conceived to be of the nature of pain and misery; and so the Self; which is the opposite of it is said to be Bliss. Therefore the concept of Pure Absolute-Existence-Consciousness-Blissful nature of Self is born out of the perception and experience of the unreal, unconscious and ever changing painful world. Thus this concept has the characteristic of an explanation by differentation.

Strictly speaking, Self is beyond definition. Because speech cannot express it, mind cannot think it, intellect cannot understand it, nor any other mode of perception can apprehend it; for all these faculties are of the nature of effects. Only those things can be defined which are limited by space, time and/or object. As Self is beyond all limitations, it cannot be defined. If we insist on being given a definition of Self, appproximating to it and yet true, then we can state that it is Supreme Existence, supreme consciousness and supreme bliss. Because the world is unreal like the snake seen in the rope, inert like a pot and painful like poison; while the Pure Self is real like the rope, self luminous like the sun and blissful like nectar. Thus there being no limiting adjuncts it is also perfect and pure, total-freedom and knowledge.

Now, here a question arises, Is it possible to perceive such a knowledge? Is there any such non-mediate perception that is experienced as Self-Knowledge called as Self-Realization? For this we have to deal in brief about perception, which is done in the next chapter.

7

An Analysis of Perception

In brief let us have a description of perception according to Sanatana Method. Perception is a process of the consciousness to apprehend an object. It is one of the means of valid knowledge in the world and consists of an inseparable relation of the perceptive consciousness with its content. The objects that are seen in the world are considered by the common man to be existing outside one's body and the senses; and he feels that the objects are reflected, as they are, in his mind and in perception. The object itself does not enter any sense organ but there is a transmission of vibration in a wave form from the object, with which a person's consciousness comes in contact, which thereby becomes a content of his consciousness and on account of which he is said to know the existence of the external object. This perception is caused by the operations of the mind whose existence as a mediator between the Empirical Self within and the object outside is evident from the fact of the synthesis of sensations and of the possibility of the abscence of perception at certain times. Therefore sense-knowledge is the product of the connection between the Empirical Self, mind, the sensory organs and the object. That is why there is no simultaneity of the knowledge of the impressions received through the various sensory organs. The impossibility of simultaneity of knowledge through various sensory organs is experienced by everyone- 'My mind was else where, I did not see that', this implies the existence of the mind, i.e., the internal organ. It is due to the attention and non-attention of this internal organ (mind), perception and non-perception takes place. This mind in not an integral whole but it has parts and it can move in space. It is a changing and differentiating thing. Its going out to an object and taking its shape is actual. The mind, in particular, is always undergoing conscious and unconscious modifications. The mind is a radiant, transparent and light-substance, thus it can travel outside like a ray of light through any sense-organ. The mind is thus a specific active force, a form of the general all pervading active force. The mind is not something passive, static and merely receptive as viewed by some Western Philosophers. But it takes an active part in perception both by reason of its activity and the nature of that activity as caused by its latent tendencies. So the radiant mind goes out through any sense organ upto the place where an object is, and gets transformed into the shape of the object. This modification of the mind is called as a vibration i.e. a wave (vritti.).

The sensations are first converted into percepts by the mind, which then presents these percepts to the intellect. The intellect converts these percepts into concepts or ideas. Just as crude sand is turned into beautiful glassware of various sorts in a glass factory, similarly mere sensual vibrations are turned into powerful ideas or concepts of various descriptions in the factory of mind-intellect duo. Thus the external senses are only instruments in the process of perception. The real auditory, tactile, visual, gustatory and olfactory centres are in the brain and in the astral body. These centres of brain are the real-senses which make perception possible. The intellect receives material from the mind and presents them to the Self. As soon as facts are placed by the intellect before the Self, there flashes out the Ego. The intellect receives back the message as if, reflected from the Self, then decides and also determines before transmitting it to the mind for the execution of the deeds and needs. The external organs of action carry out the orders of the master, the Empirical Self.

The inner psychical instrument i.e., internal organ (Antah-Karana) is a broad term which includes the intellect, the ego, the memory, the sub-conscious mind and the conscious mind. Being one it assumes all these names due to its different functions.

In ordinary persons the mental images are distracted and undefined. Every thought has a name and an image, a form or a shape. Whatever one sees outside has its counterpart in one's mind. The limited sense-organs are able to cast the image of an extensive scene on the limited mind working in body on account of the essentially omnipresent and all comprehensive character of the consciousness that is reflected through the mind. All perceptions imply the marvellous working of this immanent consciousness through the instrumentality of the mind, and later through the senses. The real seer and the senser of things is this consciousness which is at the background of the perceiving subject and the perceived objects as their existence and essence. Thus the ultimate knower of the world is an absolute Being whose presence is established by the nature of knowledge itself.

There is a striking similarity between this Sankhya theory of perception (which is close to the Sanatana method with certain differences) and the epistemological analysis made by Kant. How? According to the Sankhya system the stimulus for perception is provided by the existence of a real object outside. In right perception a real object which is outside is presented to the perceptive-consciousness. The object of right perception is not an illusion, but real, and has practical value. At first the senses give a direct apprehension of truly existent objects of which one becomes aware in right perception. The senses afford only an indeterminate perception of the object, a mere immediacy of objectivity, in the form of "This is an object". This can be said to be bare abstract perception. Concrete and determinate perception— "I know the object", takes place further inside by the inner instrument (called as Antah Karana). The mind which works with an unimaginable speed contemplates on the material supplied by the senses and gives it order and definiteness by the act of synthesis and deliberation on its part. At this stage arises the definite perception of the object as being of this kind or not this kind. Then the individual Ego (Ahankara) arrogates to itself this resultant function of the mind and transforms the impersonal perception of the mind into a personal knowledge. This empirical principle of individuality with its natural character of the unity of apperception makes the perception refer to a particular individual. The intellect decides on the nature of the perception of the ego and determines the course of action to be taken in regard to it. The understanding of the intellect is followed by a will or a determination to act. Thus the seed of one's reaction to the perceived object are sown in the consciousness of the intellect. Finally, Sankhya holds that this perception and volition are experienced by the Empirical Self-Baddha-Purusa with which the intellect is always in relation. It is the Empirical Self that gives to the intellect the power of intelligence of understanding and decision. Therefore the ultimate possibility and validity of perception is based on the consciousness of the Empirical Self.

Kant contended that self-identity is not discovered in empirical experiences, but is a condition of them. Without an *a priori* synthesis of the manifold into a unity of apperception, there is no self-identity. The 'I' of apperception, and therefore the 'I' in every act of thought, is one, and cannot be resolved into a plurality of subjects. There can be in us no modes of knowledge, no connection or unity of one mode of knowledge with another, without a basal unity of conciousness which precedes all data of intuitions, and by relation to which representation of objects is alone possible. This pure original unchangeable consciousness is called by Kant as 'transcendental apperception.' This transcendental unity of consciousness orders percepts into a synthetic configuration.

Even the Sanatana method (Vedanta) accepts that there is a transcendental unity of consciousness which is responsible for the experience of self-identity. The Soul is the permanent immutable Self, necessary for memory and the awareness of personal identity. Functioning as a unity of consciousness, the witness self is the presupposition of knowledge, the knower that pervades the mutable Empirical Self. The 'I' which is the background precondition of all experience, is the permanent foundational subject of consciousness that synthesizes ideas and sense data into a meaningful unity. But the difference between Kant and Samkhya from Vedanta is that the Sanatana method accepts this transcedental unity of consciousness as non-dual, Pure Existence and Absolute Bliss too; which the former never accept.

Also, according to Kant the manifold of sensations is transformed into perceptions and conceptions by the mind by means of the perceptual categories and conceptual categories with their judgement. The categories of space and time are not properties of *things-in-themselves,* but are sensible forms of intuition, which are part of the structural foundation of the mind. They are representations that underlie all intuition as *a priori* subjective conditions of sensibility, which are prior to any perception of the object. The twelve categories of understanding which are reducible to quality, quantity, relation and modality are the principal forms of thought, which contain the merely logical faculty of uniting *a priori* in one consciousness, the manifold given in intuition into coherent perceptions and conceptions. While the Sanatana view states that perception and conceptualisation are reducible to a limited number of primary categories of the mind that is the finite world is characterised by name, the internal aspect of the form and forms the external aspect of the name, analogous to the subject-object distinction. Nothing but Pure Self, can be different from name and form, since the whole of creation consists of a manifestation of name and form only. Though matter is moulded into forms with various names, yet remains as the same substance. The False Self is responsible for remembrance, recognition and so on, which are subject to mental impressions dependent on space, time and cause—the limiting forms of phenomenal existence. Thus the space, time, causation, things-in-themselves, etc. accepted by Kant are all illusory and phenomenal. This will be discussed later in detail. The perception is therefore referred to the unity of the ego and converted into personal knowledge by Kant. The intellect classsifies the perception under its categories together with those of space and time. The transcendental unity of the ego to which all experience is referred is responsible for the synthesis of Knowledge which is made available to the perceiver. In Kant, however, the order is brought about in the sensations directly by the mind or the understanding.

According to Kant all awareness involves a creative interpretation that allows understanding to occur. "If the receptivity of our mind, its power of receiving representations . . . is to be entitled sensibility, then the mind's power of producing, representations from itself, the spontaneity of knowledge, should be called the understanding". Space and time are forms of passive intuition, which are synthesized by the categories of understanding. These categories unify the diverse sense data, allowing a person to perceive the sensible objects. But according to the Sanatana view, the human observer is actively involved in the construction of the phenomenal world. In its active mode the mind projects the qualities of name and form, creating an apparent universe. The False Self and the phenomenal world of space and time are superimposed by the human mind on the

Pure True Self. The reality appears to take on the characteristics of ignorance, analogous to a conch shell being misperceived as silver. Superimposition which produces a wrong cognition of the presence of the attributes of one entity on another object, is dispelled by discriminative knowledge. Such knowledge is actually a true understanding.

While in Sankhya the manifold of sensations undergoes the process of synthesis gradually through the mind, the ego and the intellect producing an understanding. To Kant, space and time are perceptual categories but to Sankhya they are conceptual categories. Both Kant and Sankhya hold that knowledge is caused by the joint action of the senses and internal organ presided over by the intellect.

Samkhya however arrives at realism on the way of transcendental analysis and criticism. The Samkhya method in this respect has a close family likeness to Kant's transcendental method. Both start from experience, but both alike resolve experience into its noumenal antecedents and transcendental presuppositions. But these noumenal antecedents according to Samkhya, are themselves objects of a meta-psychological intuition, of transcendental divine vision, which is not admitted by Kant, so, here Samkhyan Transcendentalism parts company with Kantian Phenomenalism. We have no faculty of non-sensuous intuition, says Kant. Therefore, we have no more than a negative knowledge of the noumenal principles as per Kant. But, we are capable of a meta-empirical non-relational intuition in divine vision as per Samkhya; so we have a positive knowledge of the noumenal principles and not mere negative consciousness of them as limiting principles. The metapsychology of Samkhya is, therefore, to be distinguished alike from the critical phenomenalism of Kant.

The concept of a realistic transcedental background that is not constituted but only manifested by consciousness is common both to the Kantian and Samkhyan theories of knowledge. Common to both also, is the distinction between consciousness as the transcendental presupposition of experience and consciousness as a temporal mental event. Here Sanatana method differs, because as per Sanatana method the cognitive, cognising and objective consciousness are temporal mental event, whereas the witness consciousness, which is the

True Real Self, is not a temporal mental event. However, the analogy between Samkhya and Kant also breaks down when we come to Kant's dualism of phenomena and noumena as, Kant will not allow an extension of the forms of cognitive experience beyond the domain of phenomena. The categories, according to Kant, cannot be employed except in relation to sense-intuited data. Hence the subject of our empirical judgement is not the noumenal reality but only the phenomenal world which is categorically discontinous with its generative antecedent. We have thus no more than a negative knowledge of the noumenal principles, a positive knowledge of them requiring a faculty of non-sensuous intuition which we lack. To none of these positions does either Samkhya or Sanatana method subscribe.

Phenomenalism either in the Kantian meaning of the term or the Sanatana perspective of an unreal projection of consciousness is not admitted by the Samkhya realist. The world, for them, is a real determination of a realistic root cause, for e.g., "no man's land". This is neither an illusory qualification of consciousness nor a determination of the *things-in-themselves*. So Sankhya theory of experience is far better, as they accept a monistic becoming of an original primal matter, than to the Kantian dualism of appearance and unknowable *things-in-themselves*. Sanatana method further rectifies the Samkhyan view by accepting an illusory non-real primal matter, so that transcendence of the world would easily happen and a permanent liberation by attaining Absolute Bliss could take place.

If we compare the Sankhyan theory of knowledge with the Kantian account of experience as set forth in the critical philosophy, important differences at once present themselves in spite of some general similarity. Kant was too much engrossed in the universal and common to allow sufficient weight to the personal aspect of experience. His main task was to refute the subjectivism of the Cartesian Philosophy and the sensationalism of Berkeley and Hume which arose out of it. That the subjective or mental is itself phenomenal and therefore presupposes an affection of the *selves-in-itself* by the noumenal *things-in-themselves* is what Kant urged against every interpretation of his teaching as a rival of the older subjectivism. And the problem with which that was faced was to account for the subjectivity and the privacy of these mental states, that is, to explain the possibility of a class of objects which, while originating through the conditions of empirical objectivity in general, should yet be restricted to a single individual mind. Sankhya however with its conception of empirical reality as a multiverse and as presupposing a pluralistic illumination and manifestation of the primal matter is not faced with any of the difficulties inherent in the Kantian theory. The Sankhya theory is also not altogether free from difficulties, for example, Sankyan realism does not account for a socially shared common world, though it provides an objective personal over every individual with its individual world as the stuff of experience. Even such problem has the merit of a fullness which we miss alike in the Kantian and the Pragmatist formulations. Kant is able to secure the objectivity of experience only by ignoring the personal subjective aspects which he, in fact, is unable to restore. The defects of the Kantian statement stands out clearly in the Hegelian reconstruction of it wherein the individual including the unique and the contingent is sought to be deduced out of the Absolute idea by necessary logical process. The usual pragmatist formulations fare better than the Kantian statement in this respect. They too emphasize the personal, the individual aspects to the prejudice of the universality and objectivity of experience, representing in this respect the opposite extreme of the Kantian universalism and impersonalism. Compared with each other of these, the more carefully guarded Sankhyan statement of the problem is certainly more adequate and is much nearer to the actual facts of experience. The only perfect system is Sanatana method in which there is no defect of any kind.

One of the most important grounds on which the doctrine that sense data are distinct from physical things, owes its origin, and which, therefore, results in the contingency of the external world, is the reference of perceiving, which is a form of consciousness; to its physical, physiological and psychical conditions. This reference seems to be unavoidable in as much as perceiving is not possible except in so far as some object first acts on the percipient's bodily organism in virtue of certain physical processes, then certain physiological processes arise within his nervous system and lastly his hereditary and acquired mental make-up functions in its characteristic way. Since an object is given to perceiving through such a chain of processes, it cannot, as will easily be argued, be the same as the independently existing physical thing. Hence the plausibility of the doctrine of sense-data. But the main point here is that since our object is to construct a theory of perceiving which demands the most satisfactory understanding of the nature of perceiving we must first see whether there is any reason for going beyond the conditional character of perceiving before we actually stop at the view that perceiving is finally conditioned by a gamut of psycho-physical processes, however obvious that view may be. And, as a matter of fact, there are two important reasons which take us beyond the conditionality of perceiving—one logical and another empirical. The former is that since it is ultimately by means of perceiving that the fact of its own conditionality can be asserted, perceiving itself is unconditioned or at least, is such in one of its aspects. It might be, however, contended that act of perceiving which is conditioned and that which asserts its conditionality are separate and that the latter is in itself as much conditioned as the former. But if this argument is pressed to its farther point, it would result in an indefinite regress. From the logical point of view the acceptance of the view of perceiving as conditioned in one aspect and unconditioned in another is however preferable to the admission of regresses ad-infinitum. Perceiving, on this view indeed has a paradoxical character. But there is no way out of this position since it has not only the sanction of logical reason but is also demanded by an empirical fact which demonstrates more conclusively than mere logical reasoning; that perceiving, inspite of being conditioned is characterised by unconditionality. This fact is none other than the *compresence* of perceiving and the object perceived. No one can deny that in spite of the space that may separate the percipient from the object of his perception and inspite of all events or processes which may intervene between them, perceiving and its object, as it were, occupy a single point of space and a single moment of time. Thus perceiving is, par excellence, the point of contact between two different kinds of world, viz.,— the world of persons who happen to be the percipients and the world of impersonal things which become perceived objects on the occurence of the phenomenon called perceiving. This relation of compresence is really unique and for that reason, is indeed very difficult—its difficulty arising from the fact that it cannot be understood on the analogy of easily understandable physical relations. The metaphysical theory called Dualism as well as the various forms of the epistomological doctrine of sense-data betray the failure to realise the unique character of this *compresence*.

The above argument seems to be sufficient for the demonstration of the freedom of perceiving from physical, physiological and psychical conditions. I may mention here that two prominent western philosophers of modern times Descartes and Kant, for their own reasons, recognised this freedom of perceiving. But, as we presently see, they failed to notice that aspect of perceiving in which it is free not only from physical, psychical and physiological conditions but from all possible conditions—which freedom is really implied by '*compresence*'.

Now the discovery of the error of the view that external objects are apprehended by the percepient through the intervention of the above mentioned conditions or in other words, that knowledge is conditioned by them is not sufficient to finally obviate the erroneous doctrine of the contingency of the external world. For, there may be other ways of conceiving, an intervening medium, between the percipient and the perceivable thing and of arguing the conditionality of perceiving so that the external world may again be reduced to a contingent status. And in point of fact, at least one such is ready, widely current and consists of pressing the perceiving and its condition into a unity, with the result that perceiving comes to be viewed as an existent, and in holding that the existent event called perceiving is the intervening medium between the percipient and the perceivable thing. It must be observed here that the bare fact of perceiving, inspite of being determined by conditions which must be *existent* may not itself be existent and yet may be *real* and thus may not be an intervening medium between the percipient and the perceivable thing, since that medium must be existent and not otherwise—and that the only way to treat it as such a medium is to conceive it as an existent; which conception really follows from the view of perceiving as at once an event and the condition of that event.

It would appear at first sight that the view of perceiving as at once a *condition* and the *conditioned,* i.e., as an existent is more satisfactory than the view of it as determined by extraneous psycho-physical conditions in as much as the former does, whereas the latter does not bring out the uniqueness which perceiving really possesses and which divides it from physical events subject to the operation of mechanical conditions. But holding that perceiving is mechanically conditioned, i.e., that the external object must be given to the percipient through psycho-physical conditions, the latter view indeed reduces the external world to contingency. But since it is not necessary for it to pronounce a definite opinion in regard to the status of perceiving as such or at least it need not necessarily subscribe to the view of perceiving as mental, it may be free from the difficulty which that view may give rise to, in regard to the status of the Self that perceives, although it may even then be said to be inadequate on account of its ignorance of the question regarding the status of the Self; whereas the former view not only reduces the external world to contingency by means of its view of perceiving as an existent and therefore as an intervening medium between the percipient and the perceivable thing, but also finds itself confronted with the problem of the status of the Self in virtue of its definite view of perceiving as a form of mental existent which leaves it no option but to solve the problem in the most objectionable manner. This solution is classical and was offered by Descartes too. According to him consciousness which includes perceiving is the attribute or essence of the Self. 'Perceiving' is in point of fact, as much a temporary event in life-history of the Ego as 'being perceived' is in that of a physical thing, so by viewing 'perceiving' as the essence of the Self, Descartes really mistakes a contingent state of the Self for its concrete and complete existence and thereby reduces the Self to a contingent status. Similarly this mistake is with all other contemporary realistic theories of perceiving, for, even they are not free from the difficulties of the western traditional theories.

The critical Realists too follow Kant in correcting the mistake of **Moore** and others by holding that perceiving consists not only the subject's passive awareness of sense-data but also includes an active process, viz., believing or imagining—comprescence, as I understand it, signifies revealation of the object to the subject—which is such that it *can only be stated* but cannot be causally explained. Once the idea of its causal explanation is set on foot, the step which philosophers must take is to avail of themselves at first of the scientific concept of mechanical causation and ultimately of transcendental causation and declare that perceiving involves the subject's activity or transcendental causality. But the right course is not to make use of the causal category in any form in understanding perceiving.

I would like to suggest the following as the remedy for the difficulties of the Realists: In the first place, we must realise that knowing, perceiving or, for that matter, any other mode of consciousness, although it logically presupposes certain conditions, viz., physical, etc. . . ., is an actual fact, unconditioned, so that which is given to it may be what is in itself. I have deliberately used the word 'may' here in order to indicate that the identity of a given data with the external object would depend not only on the unconditionality of perceiving but also on what status we assign to it. This really brings in my second point. That identity which is absolutely needed for the vindication of the independent reality of the external world, would be possible provided we hold that knowing, perceiving, etc. . . ., are relations and not existents or qualities of existents. The realists of modern times indeed mention cognitive relations and yet regard knowing, perceiving, etc. . . ., as mental acts which are existents. Mental acts as existents cannot themselves be relations, but stand in need of being related to its data in virtue of some relations, which is non-existent for these philosophers. **William James** did a signal service to philosophy by first raising his doubt about the existence of consciousness (as a real pure self in its empirical form), and he was perfectly right in holding that it does not exist but failed to see that it does not exist because it is a relation. Now perceiving as a relation is unique; and on account of its uniqueness it is compresence which is qualitatively distinct from other kinds of relation.

The pecularity of relation is that while it implies relation which it relates, it does not enter into the existence of them. So according to **Alexander's** view too, the physical thing, which is given to perceiving, is no more conditioned, determined or modified by perceiving than the table which stands in the relation of co-existence with the chair, is, in anyway, affected by that relation. Thus it is the view of perceiving as relation that alone can vindicate the independent reality of the external world. This is not, however, the only purpose which this view can serve. For, on this view perceiving as relation no more enters into or affects the existence of the Self, than the existence of the external world so that the Self is an independent reality, being thus from the determination of perceiving, knowing, etc. However different our cognitive activity may be from our moral activity, they both agree in that they equally bring the Self and the not-self into relation with one another. That being so, there seems to be nothing to prevent us from arguing that cognition is characterised by the same unconditionality which Kant claims for moral activity. Kant was indeed very bold in extricating knowledge from the operation of every kind of mechanical principle, but ultimately succumbed to the influence of traditional causal conception of the knowledge in subjecting knowledge to the transcendental activity of the logical Self.

According to the **Sankhya** theory of knowledge, the validity or the invalidity of knowledge both are self-evident and does not need any external conditions to justify. These characters are inherent in the nature of knowlege itself. The **Buddhists** hold that knowledge is invalid intrinsically, but enjoys the nature of validity due to conjunction with external conditions. The **Nyaya** affirms that validity and invalidity of knowledge are both determined by external conditions and have nothing intrinsic in them. The **Minamsa** recognises, however, to a certain extent with the **Vedanta system,** i.e. **Sanatana Method,** that knowledge is intrinsically valid. Thus it cannot be validated by any other factor external to it. While the invalidity of certain forms of knowledge is due to conditions external to knowledge. Knowledge unfolds its own validity, as it is self-luminous which is made possible by its own essential nature, which, however, is not tainted by imperfection of any kind. While the determining factor in the ascertainment of invalid knowledge is the knowledge of a contradicting element or defect in the cause of the rise of that knowledge. In perception there is first the illumination of the internal organ by the consciousness, then the activation of the mind begins, which further activates the senses and thirdly the contact of the senses with the external object. In order that perception be right and not erroneous, there should be no defect either in the operation of the mind, the activity of the senses or the manner of location of the object. The presence of an uninterrupted current of an unceasing consciousness linking up these different elements contributing to perception makes right perception possible.

The Sanatana Method's theory of perception is explained by the existence of a universal consciousness in which appears the empirical distinction of subject and object mediated by a process of knowledge. According to Sanatana view the only pure reality is the absolute pure consciousness called as Self or Soul (Atman or Brahman) which is the Supreme Consciousness, and hence neither the subject nor the object nor their relation exists outside it. They are all apparent modes super-imposed on its transcendental being. This universal Consciousness is modalised into empirical perception in three ways—1. Object-Consciousness, i.e. the consciousness appearing due to the mode of the external object, 2. Cognitive Consciousness, i.e. the consciousness appearing due to the modes of the mental psychosis (Vritti) acting for cognition, and 3. Cogniting Consciousness, i.e. the consciousness appearing due to the mode of the internal organ. All these three modes are really the one universal consciousness appearing to be conditioned by object, psychosis and the internal organ itself. When the one Absolute Consciousness is conditioned (modalised) by these three relative modes valid for empirial existence, it goes by the names and the forms put on by these modes. The indeterminable Absolute becomes determined, as it were real, by the three terms of the process, all of which rise simultaneously or in order in the act of perception.

The Sanatana Method is just opposite to the Modern Medical science. Because, according to western medical science, light vibrations from outside strike the retina and an inverted image is formed there. These vibrations are carried through the optic tract and optic thalamus to the centre of the vision in the occipital lobe of the brain in the hind part of the head. There a positive image is formed. Only then we see the object in front of us. But, according to Sanatana Method's theory of perception the mind comes out through the eyes and assumes the shape of the object outside. Thus for all perceptions a psychosis (Vritti) of the internal organ is necessary, since perception is possible only when Universal consciousness is individualised by a limiting adjunct. A psychosis is a function of the internal organ and is really indistinguishable from the latter. The cognising consciousness (Conditioned by the internal organ) is said to flow out like a ray of light, which is called as cognitive consciousness (conditioned by the psychosis), upto the object outside and take the form of the object consciousness (conditioned by the object) by pervading it. This pervasion of the mental psychosis is called as Pervasion of Psychosis (Vritti Vyapti). The function of the psychosis is to cause the removal of the veil or layer of ignorance that envelops all objects (Avarnabhanga). The pervasion of the psychosis (Vritti Vyapti = VV) is the mental modification over an object in the process of perception of something external, for e.g. 'This is an object'. Whereas the pervasion of the Effect (Phala Vyapti = PV) is the consciousness of the Self which follows the psychosis in the process of perception, for, e.g. 'I perceived the object'.

In the pervasion of the psychosis (VV) over an object the derivative ignorance (Tūlāvidya) covering the object is unveiled by perceptive knowledge. The range of psychosis (Vritti) is limited and is not infinite. The psychosis that pervades an object determines only the perception of the empirical mode of an object, but does not illumine it, for it is insentient by nature. The knowledge which illuminates the perception is not a part of the mental psychosis, as the function of pervasion of psychosis (VV) is only to pervade the form of the object and cast that form in the mental mould. Thus the pervasion of psychosis has to be illuminated by the consciousness determined by the reflection of the Self in the mind. Thus it is the consciousness of the Self that illumines the psychosis, the pervasion of psychosis, the object and the act of perception, and it is the transparency of the psychosis with its proximity to the Self that makes perception possible. The resultant pervasion of the object by the consciousness through the psychosis is called pervasion of the effect PV (Phala Vyapti). for e.g. 'I perceived the object'.

The cognising consciousness (Pramātri Caitanya) moving out as cognitive consciousness (Pṛamāṇa Çaitanya) gets identified with the object consciousness (Viṣaya chaitanya) on which the object is super-imposed. This identification is possible, because the essential consciousness that underlies the cognising, cognitive and object, as their reality, is one and the same universal consciousness. The three modes are only a phenomena superimposed on the universal consciousness. Therefore the consciousness determined by the individuality of the object is appropriated to the consciousness determined by the psychosis which takes the form of the object by pervading it. This consciousness conditioned by the psychosis (vṛitti is again unified with consciousness defined by the internal organ. Then only the subject knows the objects through a relational consciousness. In abstract and indeterminate perception there is said to be only an identification of the cognitive consciousness with the object consciousness; whereas in concrete and determinate perception there is, in addition to this fact, the identification of the cognitive consciousness with the cognising consciousness. When this latter identification takes place, the egoistic individual appropriates the perception to himself and thus distinguishes it from the perception of the object by others. Though the subject and the object are spatially divided and so cannot have ordinarily any relation to each other, but still, the consciousness underlying the universe which is made manifest through the transparent internal organ by ignorance brings about consciousness of objective perception. The existence of the subject in essence is the same as the existence of the object in essence. There is one universal existence-consciousness in the whole universe, which knows itself through itself in all perceptual processes; but this truth is not explicit to the individual in bondage, due to his being overpowered by ignorance and desires. In fact, the essential consciousness in the object is not different from that in the cognitive psychosis, which again, is not different from that which is implicit in the subjective mode. The knowledge of the object is given to the subject on account of its essential identity with the object. As the consciousness of the Self is not in union with the real pure consciousness in the object, there is no intuitive perception of the identity of the essence of the object with the universal knowing subject. There is only the psychical consciousness, reflected and limited through the phenomenal mode of the internal organ which gets identified with the objective mode of object consciousness. Hence there is only objective consciousness and not unity consciousness.

The Basal or Unity Consciousness

The relation between the knower and the known in perception must be a conscious one, as any element of the unconsciousness cannot bring about knowledge of an object. And further, objects with dissimilar characters cannot mingle-(mix) with each other and become one. Hence the cause of the relation of the subject and the object in perception ought to be a basal consciousness lying as the common ground of the subject, object and their relation. Unless there is a spiritual background supporting the object, which at the same time, is also the background of the subject and its union with the object, there can be no possibility of knowledge. If there were no consciousness behind the existence of the object, there could be no contact of a conscious subject with it because consciousness does not mix with unconscious entities. Either the subject and the object are both phases of consciousness or they are mere gross physical bodies. In the former case there can be perceptive knowledge by relation, while in the latter the whole world would be in a blind darkness. But it is seen that the world is not at all shrouded in darkness, instead there is intelligence and perception. This proves that there is an independent consciousness appearing as the knower, the known and the knowledge, all at once, in the process of perception. That consciousness is itself the Basal or Unity or Pure Consciousness, also stated as Pure Reality. Thus, reality is neither the subject nor the object and their relation, but a consciousness immanent in and yet transcending the trinity.

Kant states as follows "By transcendental idealism I mean the doctrine of the appearances which are to be regarded as being, one and all, representations only, not *things-in-themselves*. All empirical objects are appearances, determined by the sensory-conceptual apparatus of the mind. Objects are empirically known as they appear in phenomenal experience and not as they are in themselves. Transcendental illusion means to equate the apparent, conditioned, determinate and sensible with the real, the unconditional, indeterminate and non-sensible". As per the Sanatana view the last part of this statement is true. But the rest is false. For *things-in-themselves* are also apparent, representations only like all other empirical objects as there is a distinction between ultimate reality and the apparent world. Because the ultimate reality and the phenomenal world exist in a relationship of reality with appearance, analogous to a rope that is misperceived as a snake. From the empirical standpoint of view only it is said that the Absolute Reality seems to create the empirical world (which includes space, time, *things-in-themselves,* etc.) by self-transformation, yet being changeless and beyond all causation. Thus, from the empirical point of view phenomenal existence is real, while from the absolute standpoint only the Pure True Absolute Self is Real and the empirical world does not exist.

This analysis of the perception gives us a clue to the understanding of the world as a whole. The world consists of experiencers and objects that are experienced, or capable of being experienced, and nothing but these exist anywhere in it. If the relation between the experiencer and the experienced is, as it has been shown, a spiritual consciousness; then there can only be a spiritual relation existing anywhere in the world. Then the world is aglow with the consciousness and is inseparable from it.

External Perception

In external perception the object is not created by the cognitive consciousness of the subject, but is only known by it as revealed through the senses. The object is a mode not of the cognising consciousness but of Pure Consciousness, which is the subtratum of even the modal appearance of the subject. Thus, the subject is on apar with the object in the degree of reality enjoyed by it. The existence of the object is rooted in the existence of the universal Pure Consciousness on which the objectness of the object is superimposed, and the existence of the subject, too, in the same consciousness on which the subjectness of the subject is also superimposed. The subject and the object are therefore one in essence. This metaphysical real identity of the ultimate realities of the subject and the object is empirically construed in ordinary sense-perception, and so it becomes in the state of individuality the cause of attachment or aversion on the part of the subject in relation to the object by way of transferring the empirical appearance of the object to the empirical appearance of the subject. Sense-perception is thus the consciousness of an identity-in-difference, a perception of the object as different from the subject, together with the consciousness of its relation to the subject by a mysterious uniting link. This identity consciousness owes its existence to the universal self, while the differensive consciousness is caused by it being modalised, restricted, and reflected in the psychosis of the internal organ. As there are many internal organs qualifying different individuals and limiting their existences, the empirical perception of individual is different from that of another, though one and the same object may become the content of the experiences of several individuals.

The internal organ cannot by its very nature apply itself to all things at once, for its operation is limited to particular objects and to certain definite given conditions. When these conditions are not fulfilled, and also when the range of the objects extends beyond the field of the operation of the internal organ functioning through the senses, there can be no real or correct perception, definite and concrete. The perceiver is not really identical with the object perceived as the two are cut-off from each other by the space-time mode which causes the natural and observable division between the empirical objects. On account of this division the individual finds it impossible to know all things simultaneously and in their true essence. Individualistic knowledge is confined to the function of the psychosis of the internal organ defining and limiting it. The objects that are perceived are not revealed in their essential constitution and reality. What we call correct perception is no doubt valid for all practical purposes in life, as it corresponds to facts that can be verified by observation, coheres with the perceptions of the different senses and with the experiences of other people, and also as it is seen to lead one to successful activity and therefore to possess the character of practical efficiency. But the objects known in empirical perception are not revealed in their true nature, for even correct perception in this sense is liable to sublation in a transcendent state. What does not allow empirical knowledge to be ultimately valid for all times is the defect in its supposed immediateness and the sensory separability of the subject and the object. The knower, in this kind of knowledge, is a reflection of the Pure Self through the psychosis of the internal organ, and so it does not correspond to the non-mediatory knowledge of the Self which is its unaffected original. The object of empirical knowledge is, likewise, a physical mode of the universal consciousness and so does not correspond to its eternal reality which is the same as the Self. Only when knowledge takes the form of an infinite self illumination as one with the Self, including the subject and all the objects, and transcending the relation of mediacy which infects all perception in the world can there be unsublatable knowledge of the true nature of things. For this, a supreme-being called as God is accepted.

According to the Sanatana view God has an instantaneous knowledge of all things in their eternal nature, for his defining adjunct is universal in its nature and is also the material cause of everything, thus containing non-mediately the roots of all things in itself. God's consciousness which is inseparably related to His power is at once the existence and knowledge of all things. Therefore God is omniscient, omnipotent and omnipresent due to His non-individualised existence.

Internal Perception

Perception is the unification of the object-consciousness and the cognitive-consciousness through the operation of the modes. The object of a mental mode may either be an external object or an internal content, something outside the mode or the mode itself. In perception the functioning of the sense organs is not essential, it is not an unavoidable condition of perception. Whether there is the operation of the senses or not, whenever there is an identity (unity) brought about between the consciousnesses particularised by the object and that modified by the mode, perception takes place. In internal perception, like that of pleasure and pain, for example, the limiting conditions of the object, i.e., pleasure and pain, and the mental mode experiencing it, get identified at one and the same place and at the same time. The unification of the object and the subject in internal perception is, as for this fact is concerned, the same as in the case of external perception. The substratum of the subject and the object in internal perception is one and the same, viz., the internal organs as modes in the universal consciousness. In the external perception of an object (as told before) the mental mode flows out through the channels of the senses to the object outside, pervades it by the pervasion of the psychosis (Vritti Vyapti) and causes the illumination of the object by lifting its derivative ignorance (Tulavidya), by means of the witness-consciousness that is illuminating the mental mode, thus bringing about the Resultant pervasion (Phala-Vyapti or conscious-perception). Whereas in internal perception the mental mode does not move out towards any object, for here the object is the mode itself with certain temporal objects like pleasure, pain, etc, directly illumined by the witness-consciousness. Internal perception is caused by mental modes (vrittis) corresponding to the modes of these percepts. But the mental modes themselves with witness consciousness are self-luminous and do not require another mode to illumine or cognise them. The assumption or introduction of some other mode for the cognition of internal modes will lead to a chain of infinite regression of modes. Therefore the mental modes should be admitted to be almost self-luminous in internal perception, capable of being cognised directly by the witness-consciousness defined by the internal organ. Pleasure and pain are known through the modes, but the latter are known immediately by the witness-consciousness through the mind. This immediate cognition of the modes (vrittis) by the witness is not without its being associated with the internal organ and its limitations. The cognition of the modes by the witness is 'immediate' in the sense that here (in internal perception) the senses are not needed as media of knowledge. The mode of pleasure or pain, for instance, is an object as well as a subject. It perceives itself non-mediately. Empirical perception can occur only of individualised objects, and so such perception is not possible either of Pure Self or mere negation or non-existence.

Here is a point to remember that **Mr. Caird** has accused Kant of not seeing the absurdity of the supposition that the synthesis by which the Self becomes conscious of itself as an object at the same time hides it from itself. Even though this is an intellectual intuition of Kant, but according to the Sanatana view Mr. Caird is also wrong as, he conceives the Self as a unity of the differences and as a circle of relations in itself. But actually this is about the false Self and not the True Absolute Self.

The Nature of the True Knowledge

Correct perception or True knowledge or Right Cognition empirically experienced is to be regarded as true when it stands the test of correspondence, coherence, and practical efficiency, and is capable of satisfying the principle of non-contradiction, otherwise it is an error.

According to the Correspondence theory, truth is a relation between an idea or a statement and its objective content. The idea or a statement of an object should correspond or agree to the content of perception. Realists hold that truth is independent of human cognition and remains unaffected by it. Reality does not depend upon our perception of it. Truth is here Fidelity to Reality, agreement with fact.

According to the Coherence theory, truth is the relation of consistency or internal coherence between all parts of our experience. Truth depends upon the harmonious constitution of consistency of the different constituents of a proposition or judgement with the parts constituting the truth. Logical coherence is the criterion of truth, and no mere agreement of idea with fact.

The *pragmatic theory* of truth depends on the *practical efficiency,* i.e. workability in experience, what leads to satisfactory consequences, what is useful in practice and life.

Truth is valid. What works as truth or satisfies us as truth is to be considered as truth for all human purposes. It is true that there cannot be correct perception unless there is a real object outside, to which our knowledge may correspond. But correspondence is not the only criterion of truth, for there can be correspondence even in the case of partial truth and errors. Correspondence has to be testified by the principle of coherence or the organic nature of knowledge, which satisfies consistently the perceptions of the different sense organs and agrees similar perceptions of the object by others. Truth also has the character of practical efficiency or workability in actual life. Though the workable need not necessarily be true, but the true is always workable. Though utility is not the exact perfect test of truth, as truth has always the utility that is unique to its nature. All these tests, however, are based on the fact of the self-evident and perfectly valid nature of one's self-consciousness. Consciousness is its own test and proof, and it exists as the basis of all proofs. The reality of the silver seen in nacre is nacre; and the reality of the nacre is the universal consciousness. Similarly the reality of dream perception is rooted in the waking consciousness of the individual, and the reality of this waking-consciousness is rooted in the pure universal consciousness. The truth of an object should correspond with its essential nature. But no human idea or concept can correspond to the reality of the Pure Self, for here no relational category can be introduced into knowledge. Empirical tests of truth cannot be applied to it, for all these tests are based on the notion of duality, while the Self is Non-dual, it is its own proof and validity, and the test of its experience is its self-evident nature. This is the only experience which is ultimately non-contradicted and so the ultimate Truth. In this, the highest being of consciousness the knower, known and knowing are one, and in it all logical tests lose their significance.

For all purposes of life, an object of correct perception by the cognising consciousness is real and has an existence of its own leading to successful activity, corresponding to empirical facts and cohering with the perceptions of others in regard to it. But it is to be added here that what satisfies these tests of truth need not be absolutely real. The world of experience, to the Vedanta i.e., Sanatana Philosophy, is, in the last resort, subject to sublation in the knowledge of the Self, to which the objects of the world cannot correspond, and in which it loses all practical efficiency, and also proves to be incoherent with the structure of the hidden and real nature of the universe. Metaphysically, and apart from what is revealed in temporal perception, all things exist in a system in which they are inter-related and mutually determined as elements ultimately compared with a supersensible completeness. Empirical judgements have only a pragmatic value, are relatively valid and sufficient for all practical purposes in one's day-to-day life. But such judgements are not ultimately valid, for all sense knowledge has to be classed under appearences, since it proceeds from the reflection of the Self in the internal organ and catches only aspects of the reality in the forms of discrete objects in space and time. Everything in the world points beyond itself to a boundless existence, and this fact is demonstrated in the constant change that things undergo, and the tendency to overcome barriers and obstructions at every step. Everything embraces all other things, for everything is a mirror reflecting the whole universe. Judgements which presuppose the isolated existences of things cannot be ultimately true, for all things exist in and for the whole. The knowledge-of the true essence of things is given not in relational perception of externalised conditions or objects, but in the non-sensuous intuitional revelation of the Absolute. Thus, the theory of perception leads to an epistemological realism, while at the same time implies a metaphysical idealism positing the existence of an absolute consciousness behind both the object and the subject. While it is accepted that the subject is in no way the cause of the existence of the object, and the object too is independent of the empirical existence of the subject, for the universe of perception reveals itself as an organic completeness containing within itself the subject and the object as elements partaking of the same level of reality, thus it is held that there is a higher reality of a spiritual nature, which comprehends and transcends the relativity of the subject and the object. On ultimate analysis it is discovered that there is nothing either in the object or in the subject except mere name and form plus the universal consciousness on which the name and form appear. Even space and time, substantiality, extension, resistance and causation etc... are all the schema of the universal knowing subject fastened on to a network of objectivity. On receiving sensations one must, truly speaking, not refer them to anything outside in space, but to the essential nature of the consciousness which is the real subject. If this is done, then there will be an experience of the instantaneous illumination of the Self as shining within and without, as subject as well as object. The rationalistic and empiricistic attitudes to perception are reconciled in the acceptance of the Self as the fundamental reality. It is the Self itself that masquerades as the seer and the seen within space-time (which are superimposed on it), and exists as the true substance behind the forms taken by the seer and the seen.

But to experience the Self in its true form as explained in the Sanatana texts (upanishads) and have a discriminative wisdom of the perception and Reality, one has to rise above the shackles of the Universe. For this, it is necessary to know the true constitution of the Universe. Is it Real or an illusion-a product of ignorance? According to most of the Eastern and

Western philosophers it is Real. Until and unless there are two realities, Universe and Self, none can overcome miseries and bondage. Thus it is necessary to briefly discuss and decide about the constitution of the universe, which is being done in the next chapter.

8

The Universe and its Constitution

The term Universe signifies the totality of space, time and matter. Modern physical science has discovered that matter has no independent existence but can be reduced to the ultimate constitution of the space-time manifold. In general, space is conceived as extendedness with three dimensions, and time as a consciousness of the succession of events in space. Thus, common-perception makes an empirical distinction between space and time. But scientists like Einstein, Eddington, etc., have tried to demonstrate and prove that every event in the universe has a four-dimensional character. What we perceive is not just space and time but a space-time continuum. Matter is found to owe its origin to a particular feature discoverable in the space-time manifold. A kink or twist or curvature in space-time is said to be responsible for the appearance of what is commonly called matter. The nature of this kink is dependent upon the quality and the amount of matter that it contains. The greater the matter, the greater is the kink. This kink is that which is called by the name "gravitational force".

But philosophers like Kant denied any externality to space and viewed it as a necessary mode of objective perception, a special condition of the sensibility. Space, however, is not a creation of any individual mind, for all perceptions are contained in it, though it is possible for us to believe that space may be a mode of perception by a cosmic mind. In these days, there is a tendency to reduce perceptual space to certain kinds of relationship between bodies, to position, distance and direction. Even those relations are external, objective and real to all perceiving minds and are not the creations of any particular mind. Space, thus is a cosmic factor necessary for the perception of things by all minds. Similarly, time appears to be a very necessary element in the understanding of any event either abstractly or completely. It is not enough to know just the three dimensions—right and left, up and down, near and far—related to any object or event. We also need to know a fourth dimension, i.e., succession in terms of before and after. Such temporal succession in space is called Time. Due to the peculiar manner of the reactions of our minds to events that occur in space which we call as succession, we are forced to create distinction between past, present and future. The succession is really continuous, and no genuine demarcation can be made in it. But according to the working of our minds in the form of sense perception, memory and imagination, the three fold distinction is made in the passage of Time. In fact, the present is only a concept. It does not exist as distinguished from the past and future. In actual practice the present turns out to be the subtle concept of an infinitesimal part of the succession of events, which directly appears as a content of sense experience. The past has an infinite history and the future has infinite possibilities, while the present fades away either to eternity or nothingness.

Space, time and matter have a common-origin which contains all these in a unified and a homogeneous form which is designated today as the space-time-continuum. The **Newtonian** conception of absolute space and time with localised bodies in them has been abandoned, while the concept of gravitation has undergone a new orientation. Matter also is fast losing its solidity and is being accepted to be an indescribable energy, which is now considered to be the matrix of the universe. According to Einstein and his followers, the ultimate physical reality of the universe is space-time continuum. The inequalities, the twists, the curved nature of space-time constitute the visible matter. This means that matter can be reduced to energy and the space-time manifold. Newton's theory which states that material bodies are drawn out of the straight line which would be their natural course of motion, in the direction of other material bodies by a peculiar force called gravitation; has been now supplemented by the discovery that no such force exists and bodies are not pulled but that what is called as the gravitational force is nothing but a peculiar curvature of space around bodies of matter. Thus the stable universe of Newton has disappeared into a cosmos of relativity with space-time as its ultimate basis, constructed out of waves of energy and intervals of events. There are no objects, only events; no points of space, only waves of energy. The visible universe is therefore not the real one. In the modern physicist's view the real universe becomes a supersensible object. Even though we are given a hard, tangible and visible universe with the qualities conveyed by our senses a universe of mathematical point-events, symbols, etc..., which in the end clamour for being reduced to nothing but thought. To **James Jeans,** the universe is a construction of a cosmic mathematical mind, which may be called God. But to **Arthur Eddington,** the universe is of the stuff of a cosmic mind or consciousness. An enquiry into the ultimate reality of the physical universe has ended practically in a negation of it by the most advanced scientists of the day, and have returned to mind and consciousness as its reality. Physics has thus landed itself into metaphysics, and the scientist has become a semiwise philosopher. Matter is slowly disclosing its essential psychical and spiritual Being. Surely in future everybody will accept the Sanatana philosophy that universe is an illusion, superimposed on the Absolute Self.

Space is the condition of externality and time the process of continuance of being. We know the World as contained in space and as existing in time. There is no world without space and time, and no idea of our living as human beings can ever arise except for in terms of space and time. These two are fundamental for all experience, and life is unimaginable without the conceptions of extension and period. It would appear from the nature of things that a knowledge of space and time would necessarily provide an insight into the nature of the world as a whole. The importance of this proposition becomes evident when we envisage the utter imposssibility of the very concept of being, as far as we are concerned, except on the presupposition of the idea of space and time. Even thought becomes abortive when it is forced to operate without the postulation of these limiting conditions prior to the attempt at thinking, or atleast simultaneously with it. The world is often identified with the time process and is indistinguishable from the notion of mass and dimension. Perhaps the world is what we understand by space and time, when we can define and explain them. So, what are space and time? Are they absolutely real and identical with absolute truth, the non-dual superconsciousness, the Self? The answer is 'No'.

The book Yoga Vasiṣṭha abounds in an extensive treatment of the nature of the world in terms of space and time, propounds the amazing doctrine that space and time are not realities in themselves but are appearances relative to experience. It teaches that space and time are constructions of thought and are dependent on thought. One cannot conceive of space and time, when the functions of the mind are inhibited, or when no consciousness seems to operate.

It is possible for different persons existing in different orders of reality to experience the same world as being possessed of different space-time significance. The reality of space and time, and also the stability, order and meaning of the things of the world change, in different space-time realms. There can be no experience of space or time without the conditioning of the Pure Consciousness. Space is a mode of perception by the individualised observer. Thus the perception of space is relative to the activity of the mind. Under different conditions, different orders of space can be perceived by the same mind. Even a small area of space can appear to the mind, under certain circumstances, as a vast kingdom. For example, the mind in the state of dream experiences a universe with its own space and time. The dream world has all the characters and structual qualities of the waking world and yet the two realms are totally different from each other. We also know that, even in this waking world, the mind can perceive a thing as what it is not. The mind can project forth space in accordance with the condition in which it is. The idea of time, is dependent on the idea of space. In fact, the concepts of space and time rise simultaneously, and as spatial characters are relative to states of mind, so are time characters too. Whatever is the nature of the objective condition to which consciousness is related, that alone appears to it as reality. When consciousness accepts the idea of a moment, even an age can be passed as a moment, while, when it is identified with the idea of a long period of time, even a moment can be experienced as an age. Therefore the nature of experience of space and time depends upon the manner in which the consciousness happens to be objectively modalised. Persons who are in a depressed state of mind or who are in deep sorrow are able to feel that a moment of time is like a year, while those who revel in happiness would feel the contrary. In the state of intense spiritual contemplation and *samadhi* (total introvertness with a non-triune state), space and time are transcended, and only Pure-Consciousness reveals itself. Therefore space and time are ultimately conditions of consciousness and are not independent of it. Space is the way in which the mind knows things as having extension, and time is the feeling of the succession of internal states reacting to those of events outside.

The relativity of space and time, the ultimate ideal character of the world and the presence of worlds within worlds are picturesquely illustrated by many remarkable stories in the Yoga Vāsiṣṭha. The gist is as follows:

1. The worlds exist within worlds, interpenetrating but without affecting one another. The one is absent... to the other, though the one may exist within the other. But one who wishes to have a knowledge of the other worlds, may, by extraordinary powers, obtain it.

2. Even many worlds, can exist in an atom, because space and time are not limited to any single order of perception. There are different spaces and times and there are different worlds of different kinds, each governed by the special laws of its own space and time.

3. The events that take place in a moment in a particular world may occur in a long universal cycle in some other world. In dream, one may experience the vicissitudes of a whole life in a moment. The same rule applies to other worlds also.

4. All our experiences are the results of our beginingless desire-impressions. One's birth, death and the environment in which one lives are all the direct consequences of one's own desires.

5. There is no such thing as static and unconditioned world which can be valid for all people and for all times except for Pure-Absolute Bliss.

6. Each one's world is made out of his own desires, though the material of that world may be drawn from any objective realm which may be equally real to many others who, too, happen to be born in that world due to the similarity of conditions which they are expected to experience.

The Philosopher 'Kant' thought that space and time are empirically real and transcendentally ideal. The ideas of space and time are, according to him, required to give form and order to the manifold of sensations which are not presented in an orderly form. Space and time are perceptual categories, they are the necessary conditions of all perceptions. Space is said to represent and determine the form of external perception, while time represents and determines the perception of internal states. They are *empirically real,* for they constitute not mere forms of perception but actual perceptions themselves. They are the sense-data which, with the structure of the understanding, make all definite human knowledge possible. They are *transcendentally ideal* for they are ultimately *a priori* forms of perception and are contributed somehow by the nature of the sensibility and the understanding. The view of Kant thus seems to be that space and time have a meaning only from the point of view of individuals, though they are universal in the sense that they are valid for other minds also.

Thus Kant noted that "empirical objects" are therefore real if they stand in an empirical connection with any actual consciousness, although they are not for that reason real in themselves". Phenomenal objects are no mere illusions. For in an appearance the objects, nay, even the properties that we ascribe to them, are always regarded as something actually given. Both space and time are phenomenally real but transcendentally ideal, since they do not apply to *things-in-themselves*. But as per the Sanatana view the whole phenomenal world is an illusion, an appearance or representation. As the ignorance or primordial stuff (Maya) is ineffable and indefinable, neither real nor unreal. It (Maya) is not real since it cannot exist apart from Consciousness independently, and this inert ignorance is negated when the absolute consciousness is realised. It (Maya) is not even an absolute illusion analogous to the son of a barren woman, since it is responsible for the world of appearance and is pervaded by the absolute reality. From the practical standpoint the universe is phenomenally real, but is not ultimately real.

On the other hand, for Kant, the limits of possible human knowledge are due to the inherent *a priori* limitations of sensibility and the conceptual categories of the mind. Space and time are infinite, yet objects are known only through specified limitation. Space is essentially one; the manifold in it and therefore the general concepts of spaces, depend on limitations. Similarly, every determinate magnitude of time is possible only through limitations of a single time that underlies it. Thus understanding is not limited by sensibility, on the contrary, it itself limits sensibility. But actually, as per Sanatana view, the phenomenal existence (even of space and time, along with *things-in-themselves* is a limitation of the ultimate reality, the Pure Absolute Self, conditioned by restricted mental forms of the human mind. The limiting adjuncts are expressed through a mental mode taking a subjective form as internal cognition and an objective mode as external perceptions. The finite adjuncts of the mind and senses appear to limit, individualise and divide the infinite, confining to a particular space and time. The individual self is a particularised qualification of the Absolute Consciousness. Remove the conceptual and perceptual restrictions of name and form, then the individual becomes one with the Absolute. So, according to Sanatana method even the understanding is a limited phenomenal substance.

But the absolute character of space and time has been denied by the physical theory of relativity. The three dimensional space and the one-dimensional time which were supposed to have absolute validity have now been found to be welded together into a primordial stuff of space-time, of which the space and time which we ordinarily know are mere abstractions. The real physical world is therefore, a four-dimensional realm with the ideas of up and down, right and left, forward and backward, and before and after for its constituents. These four sets of relations are to be taken into consideration in determining the character of a particular event. The theory of relativity has further led to modify our conception of matter which, it holds, is not an independent entity by itself, but is constituted of twists and turns or wrinkles in the space-time manifold. Space and time are discovered to be relative to the position and motion of the observers and systems of reference they employ. When these systems change, the significance of space and time also changes accordingly. The significance is however, universal and not merely individual. This position has been summed up by **James Jeans,** thus : "Thus we conclude, with a high degree of probability, that the space-time unity and the objects which figure in it cannot be mere constructs of our individual minds, but must have existences of their own, although we know that space and time separately are just abstractions of our minds from the space-time unity. But this does not, of course, touch the question-time and the material world are or are not of a mental nature, being perhaps the constructs of a consciousness superior to our own. So long as we are concerned with only our sensations, it is all the same, whether we regard the world as a mental construct or as having an existence of its own, independent of mind—the essential point at the moment is that it cannot be a private mental construct of our own".

Besides, the fact that space and time are mental constructs need not neccessarily mean that each individual experiencer should have an absolutely independent world. There can be a common space-time for all observers who happen to use the same system of reference, though there may be differences in the manner of their subjective reactions and interactions in relation to other individual of the same space-time world. This shows that the external world of common experience is not a construction of any particular individual but is the uniform object—with exceptions of subjective reactions—experienced by a number of individual minds, establishing thus an existence of itself with some sort of independence on the perceiving minds. But even the world of a common space-time to different individuals or frames of reference must fall within the construction of a cosmic mind which should include all subjects and objects of perception. Thus the space-time world is extramental to the individual experiencers, but mental to the cosmic experiencer. But from the point of view of the ultimate consciousness, the ideality of the world of space-time is revealed, and this ideality has reference and validity only to this consciousness. And as this consciousness is universal, the world of space-time is ideal only to it and not to the individuals. The latter are bound to particular and relative forms of reference of space-time. This bondage is the cause of birth and death cycle. The universal consciousness, on the other hand, is the single witness and observer of the totality of all space-time references and, not being confined to any particular order of space-time, it is eternally liberated and is identified with freedom and bliss.

The Yoga Vāsiṣṭha demonstrates the truth that the same event can have several dates and locations. Therefore an event that may take place for us on a particular day or date in a particular place (space-time) need not necessarily mean that it is completely restricted to that particular space-time coordinate for observers who happen to use to different system of reference. Thus every event is a universal event and is valid to the whole cosmos, though with the necessary changes required to make it relevant to the realm of being which is valid to all frames of space-time experience. It is on this basis that in the famous, and biggest-epic of the world 'Mahabharata', to answer any question one past event is revealed in present context. This is the *'Sanatana'* Method of establishing human values. As the past, present and future have no absolute determinations but are significant only in relation to individual experiences, any event, taken by itself and at a single given moment of time, may belong to either the past or the present or the future in accordance with the space-time coordinate from which it is viewed. And from the point of view of the universal being, an event is a universal process inseparable from the consciousness in which it occurs as it is due to the primordial stuff (Maya). The divisions of space and time are, therefore, not truths having any real meaning to all experiences but are, in a sense, working hypotheses constructed for making individual life possible. Thus space-time is a relation and not an existence. This world of space-time in which we live is not the only possible or the real one. There are as many worlds with as many space-times as there are frames of reference for modes of consciousness. When freed from the limitation of any particular frame of space-time, an event reveals its character of being universal, without spatial or temporal confinement of any kind. An event is infinite and eternal if only it can be extricated from particularized space-time references. As truth is a universal oneness, all events in all space-times should be contained in it as non-different from it.

The Phenomenal Character of Space

A knowledge of space implies a knowledge of the terms that it relates, and a knowledge of these terms, again, requires a knowledge of space that differentiates them. Space and the things that it relates determine one another. It is not true that space and time have an existence independent of the bodies which they contain and limit. If there is no individual existence, there is no spatial existence, also. Our dream perception is the best example: space and time with the objects appear to be all real while they are seen, but, on waking, the dream's space and time vanish together with the dream objects. We do not see the dream's space and time persisting even when their objects are being contradicted in waking. Thus space and time are inseparable, related to their contents, and their contents, again, are inseparable from space and time in which they are involved. Without spatial and temporal distinction there is no objectness. This shows that what we perceive is not merely an isolated object but a complex system of reference which determines the nature not only of the object of knowledge but also of the individual constitution of the knower. The threefold process of the relation among the knower, known and the knowledge, is involved in a particular space-time reference which determines the nature of all the three elements in the process. The greatest error that is committed in all our objective researches and endeavours is that we disregard the role that is played by ourselves in our activities. What we know is really not any independent object but a complex situation in which the object is involved. And in this situation we ourselves as knowers are involved, so that in the degree of reality's manifestation in the form of subject and the object of our knowledge is equal, that means there is practically no difference. Therefore all quest for genuine knowledge must pay due regard to all the factors that are implicit in the manifestation of empirical knowledge. Duly every act of knowledge includes the characters of space, time, causality, individuality and a distinction between the knower and the known. Real knowledge is always a whole, and it binds together, in an internal-external relation, all the constituents which bring it about. This phenomenon gives us a very clear insight into the truth that we live in, not only as private individuals but as the inhibitants of a cosmos where each is related to the other in the manner of parts to the whole in a living organism.

It is thus decided that space is not an ultimately real stuff from the fact that externality is not ultimately real. Externality is the same as duality in perception, and reality is ever free from it, for what is real is never known as an object or external to oneself. Thus when externality is not real, space also cannot be real. Therefore reality of space is there only as long as externality is recognised as a fact. An inward harmony among things, which is their ultimate essence, discloses the empirical character of space and time. Discreteness among objects is fundamental to space and indivisibility is natural to reality. That space and time are appearances is discussed by **Prof. Taylor** on metaphysical grounds too—"An absolute experience must be out of time and out of space, in the sense that its contents are not apprehended in the form of spatial and temporal series, but in some other way. Thus Space and time should be the phenomenal appearance of a higher reality which is spaceless and timeless".

The Transcendence of Space in the Self

The world of space and time has no independent existence but it is an illusion super imposed on the Supreme Self. The Self is the absolute pure reality, while the space-time world has only pragmatic reality relevant only to empirical experience. Space has a meaning in the distinction that is commonly made between in and out, here and there, this and that, etc . . . This distinction obtains validity only so long as there is no recognition of the true relation that subsists between the two points related. The ultimate ground for relation among things is pure-consciousness, independent of objects, and the non-experience of it is the condition for the perception of spatial difference. The differentiation of the knowing Self from its object is the prerequisite of the appearance of space. The moment the Self is segregated from the contents of its knowledge, there is the notion of space and time arising in it. In the undivided consciousness of the Self, the distinctions—in and out, etc. . . gets merged; and space, whose essence in this distinction gets negatived. For the same reason, temporal distinction has no meaning to the Self, for the Self is that consciousness which knows even this distinction. Thus the division of time into the past, present and future has a spatial import, and the non-spatial Self ought to be non-temporal too. While the time-series is to be identified with a state of change, the Self which witnesses all changes is known to remain changeless. For all changes are appearances consequent upon the false isolation of the Self from the objects, and vice-versa. The agency of Self in action, and the validity of action, also, are based on this erroneous notion of the individualisation of consciousness as separated from its objects. The knowledge-essence of the Self becomes evident only when its spatial embodiment and temporal conditioning are known to be unreal. The individuality of the individual, the plurality of the selves and the diversity of objects are all trascended in the oneness of the Self. The whole of the world consists of confinement to space-time, for it arises on account of the misconception that the body or mind, etc., is the Self, this misconception is simultaneous with the rise of the notion of space and time. The essence of Self is knowledge and this knowledge has no distinctions—in and out, etc., for it is universal. Therefore the Kathopanishad declares that—whatever is here is also there, and whatever is there is also here, and that, he goes from death to death who perceives here diversity, as it were. In pure consciousness there is no plurality or duality, and so no space or time. Cāndogyopaniṣad states—The Self is alone below, above, front, back, to the right, to the left; the Self indeed, is all this.

Time is also an Appearance

Time is also a false thing. It is a mode of the mind. It is a mental creation. It is a trick or jugglery of the mind. Time is an illusion. In dream, within ten minutes, you see events of a hundred years. Even in wakeful state, if you are concentrated, three hours appear as half an hour; when the mind is restless, half an hour also appears to be more than three hours. Therefore we can boldly state that time is non-external and non-eternal but an illusion like space. All things in this world acquire a meaning when they are understood in terms of their existence in time, and shorn of all relevance to it, they have no significance. Every object or event in this world is at once connected with a past and suggests a future, though it has also a present. Nothing can merely exist in the present without reference to a past and a future. A present without a past or a future is totally inconceivable to us. Time has a speciality, that individuals have no power to move in it, though they have an ability to move in space. This is why there is a desire in all beings to perpetuate their existence and their actions, reflecting thereby the presence of an eternal something which is their ultimate ideal. Things in this world of time do not exist but flow in a series of events. That means the world is not Being but becoming. Time is becoming, while eternity is Being. Tomorrow becomes today and today becomes yesterday. The future becomes the present and the present becomes the past. A thing that is becoming, changing, cannot be eternal. These temporal events, as viewed from the standpoint of the eternal, are not externally related bits, but a mirroring of the Absolute. As far as ordinary experience is concerned the consciousness of time cannot be separated from the consciousness of space. Because whatever we know is not only in time but also in space. Thus space and time are not two different realities conditioning our experiences in different ways, but appearances or aspects of one reality. Modern Science calls this matrix as space-time continuum or a four dimensional continuum. The truth of individuality lies not in itself alone, but in the complex structure of the total experience constituted of different factors, viz. space, time, selfhood, object, etc. We always think and believe ourselves to be in space and time, and never in a space-time unity, for, to think in a space-time unity would mean not to think at all as individual beings.

Causation—A Law of Necessity

The human mind is bound up in the idea of causal relation. The cause seems to precede the effect in a temporal sequence. It is impossible for us to think of the occurrence of events independently of the concept of causality. Because space, time and cause are the three basic units of all conceivable knowledge. The moment an event or effect is known, it is found to be in space and time, and is at once linked with others in a causal change. We are accoustomed to think that there ought to be a cause for every effect and that every effect should be related to its cause spatially and temporally. The common sense view of this causality, however, does not stand the test of careful scrutiny. On observation it is found that every cause has another cause behind it, so that no single object or event can be considered to be a cause of any particular effect. There is a series of causes, even as there is a series of effects. If we take into consideration the position of an event in this long chain of causation, we will find that every cause is also an effect with reference to that from which it has originated, and is a cause in relation to that which originates from it. Further, no single factor does ever become a cause of any condition or situation. The truth is that, the ordinary view of causation takes only a bit of the whole process by way of abstraction, disregarding the other factors which are not open to the immediate observation of the senses and the mind. Thus the question that arises now is—as to whether causation is a fact relevant to the world in itself, or it is only a mental habit to cognise events in a particular way.

Kant holds that mind imposes on the chaotic and disorderly material of the world its own laws of order, regularity, causality, etc., so that our experiences must fit in with the framework of the mind. This framework is also set by the mind for the arrangement of objects which become the contents of its knowledge. Things of the world for ex: a pot, a cloth, a table etc., in themselves, i.e. seen as a pot, seen as a cloth, seen as a table etc., are not really related exactly in the way in which the mind supposes them to be; but the recognition of causation in the world of events is a necessary condition of the mind, to be obeyed and fulfilled, if we are to have any experience.

Modern Physics maintains that the mind selects certain aspects of the world, which can fit into the categories of which it is constituted, and rejects other aspects which remain outside its knowledge. Therefore the symbolic world of present day physics is an abstraction of a mental construct from reality, and this abstraction obeys the laws of the mind, of mathematics and of physics.

Thus the conclusion is as arrived by Eddington that—"Where science has progressed the farthest, the mind has but regained from nature that which the mind has put into nature." That means to say that we seem to discover ourselves in the world outside.

What is Causal Relation?

Causation implies that one thing proceeds from another thing with a definite relation. Two totally different things cannot be cause and effect, as for, they have unrelated independent existence. But if there is a relation, then there is no sharp difference too between cause and effect. The discovery of the nature of the effect in the cause shows that cause and effect are, essentially, non-different. And if they are non-different, there can be no causation, for causation has a meaning only when cause and effect have some sort of essential independent difference as well as some sort of similarity too. Thus the causal concept is logically indefensible, as it arises on account of our compassion to the notion of the spatialisedness of experience. No intelligible explanation can be offered for causation on the basis of the belief in the separation of objects from one another.

At the best our worldly experiences makes us aware of a rapid and temporal succession of changeless and non-temporal facts, if such a thing were possible. It would in other words make our experience discrete and discontinuous and then there would not be any idea of change and even of time, as Kant so conclusively demonstrated against Hume. Change implies causality. I do not see any sense in which, on this view, causal connections can be made intelligible or shown to be more than succession. Causality implies identity. To say that anything has a cause is to assert that the thing in its present aspect does not explain itself, is not self-subsistent. In order to explain its appearance in the present we have to carry it back to the past and show that the present is intelligible in the light of its past existence, i.e., is consistent with it. The present in explaining itself, transcends itself as the purely present and asserts that it has the roots of its being contained in the past. If we do not admit this then in what sense does the past explain the present? The shifting sense data cannot explain each other because they have nothing in common. Any sense data can be brought forward to 'explain' any other. What is truly explained is shown to be no new fact—what is wholly new does not admit of explanation. As Kant asserts, objective time determination is possible only throuh the concept of causality, and causality must mean actual transformation, analogous to Milk converting to Curd (Yogurd). So causality is introduced merely to give us the assurance that in the two successive perceptions that we have, the object remains the same, that there has been change *in* the object rather than *of* the object. Nothing is not which once was and nothing was not which once is.

Briefly the Sanatana doctrine of causality is as follows—Effect is identical with the cause and yet with certain aspects of its own it distinguishes itself from the cause, otherwise causation will have no meaning. It is in a sense a new product and yet not new. In short the effect as such has an inexplicable existence, it escapes all logical determination, analogous to the ornaments of Gold. Thus all our experiences instead of trying to explain in terms of causality it would be better to negate it like the snake on the rope. The duality that hampers us at every step becomes a great hindrance in bringing out a correct understanding of life in its true sense. **Prof. James Jeans** says—"If we suppose that happenings of nature are governed by a causal law, then we must suppose that the cause of any effect is the whole previous state of the world, so that every effect has an infinite number of causes." So those who have no trust in the Sanatana view's great treatise Yoga Vasiṣṭha, for such Kantians, I would like to draw their attention on to the illustration given by **Prof. C.E.M. Joad** in his "Guide to Philosophy." Starting with the explanation he says that, "An observer sitting in a comet travelling away from the earth and viewing events occuring upon the earth through a telescope will be able to observe the events of the earth when the light rays travelling from the earth reach him, he says that, If the speed of the comet were equal to that of light—then the events occurring on the earth would cease to appear to the observer, since no light rays carrying the message of the events can catch him. And if, again, the velocity of the comet were to exceed that of light, the observer will see the sequence of events in reverse order. Because he will catch up the light rays travelling from the earth which convey the message of events first than those of the cause. Therefore what we call causes will appear to him as effects and our effects will be to him causes". The purport of this illustration is that the idea of cause and effect is not valid to the events themselves, but that is dependent upon the point of observation, and that the directive of causation is relative to the position and velocity of the observer. Thus causation reduces itself to a mental construction, a form of perception and understanding, which is further totally empirical. That means to say, the world of causation cannot be the real world; the real must be other than what we know through the instruments which we are endowed with.

Arthur Eddington introduces a distinction between causation and causality. "Causation is that relation of cause and effect in which there is the notion of the temporal antecedence of the cause to the effect". But by causality Eddington does not mean temporal sequence of events valid to the observing minds, instead he terms it as "a symmetrical relation of the totality of the events forming the world, in which the world is conceived of as a complete system of inter-connected events". **Whitehead** also holds a similar view to it proposing a reality of the nature of an organic process. However, we have to add that, causality can be said to be objective only in the sense that it is observed not merely by one mind but by all minds. But still it remains a fact that both causation and causality are meaningful only to minds and that its extramental validity cannot be established. Even though we are obliged to admit that causality may be the way of a cosmic mind due to which it enjoys an independent existence outside individual minds. But the purely hypothetical character of this supposition cannot be denied. *"A necessity of thought need not be an uncontradictable truth"*. **James Jeans** observes that—"If we still wish to think of the happenings in the phenomenal world as governed by a causal law, then we must suppose that these happenings are determined in such a substratum of the world, which lies beyond the world of phenomena, and so also beyond our access". The Sanatana view states this substratum to be the Self only, as all phenomena is a super-imposition on the Self.

Causation among things outside is to be understood as the individualistic reading of the consequences of an indivisible consciousness appearing as the witness of objects which have it as their existence and content. The function of this universal principle as an unbroken continuum appears, when it is manifest in individuals, as the law of causation and causality among things and events. The dynamic self-expression of the Absolute in the world of objects involves a causal relation among them. Thus, causation has a meaning in the empirical world only and is meaningless to the Absolute.

9

How *Sanatana* View Can Correct 'Kant'

We have discussed enough, in general, different topics and shown the way in which science and western philosophy should be dealt with by Sanatana view. Now let us discuss on Kant directly and correct him by Sanatana view. For that let us go through Kant briefly.

Immanuel Kant is said to have been woken up by Hume from his "dogmatic slumber" and brought a 'Copernican revolution' in the field of Philosophy. In Kant we begin to reap the ripe fruits of western philosophy, for it is here that, it seems western philosophy has reached maturity and full development.

Kant discovers that neither empiricism nor rationalism is entirely correct, though each is partially true. His problem is therefore to take stock of the previous findings in philosophy and to construct his own critical philosophy or transcendental idealism. Kant begins by saying that knowledge is not completely derived from sense-experience. We cannot confine our knowledge to the senses, as Locke and Hume supposed. Hume committed the mistake of restricting experience to separate and distinct sensations, and from this false premise came to the false conclusion that there is nothing necessary or universal in knowledge. Sense-experience gives us only probabilities and not certainties. If there is a certain, necessary and universal knowledge, it must be independent of sense-experience. The necessity and universality about such knowledge is true was prior to sense-experience, it is *a priori*. We have in mathematics, knowledge, which are necessary and universal, they are unaffected by what experience the senses may give us in the course of time. For never in this universe an addition of five and seven would cease to make twelve. This is an example of knowledge independent of sensations. Here, Kant is a dogmatist. Because instead of asking whether synthetic judgements a priori **are** possible, he takes for granted that there is already such knowledge, and concerns himself with **how** synthetic judgement, *a priori* are possible.

Kant's method can be summarised as follows:

(i) He starts from the indubitable of *a priori* synthetic judgements in arithmetic, geometry and physics. This being a present indubitable fact whatever is required for its constitution must also be granted. It may be noted that he never doubted either the synthetic character of these propositions nor their existence, and hence the question that he propounded to himself in the 'critique' was not whether the said propositions were synthetic or existent, but only 'how they are possible', i.e., which hypothesis would secure such results.

(ii) Therefore as the second step we may mention, he considered the alternative already in the field-empirical generalisation and analytical concept, and ruled them out on their own and accepted of character of *'a posteriority'*, and lack of syntheticity. His arguments regarding space and time are cases in point.

(iii) Thirdly, it is not possible to refer these to either things-in-themselves or their determination or relations, for in that case they cannot be known and predicated *a priori*—as the said propositions undoubtedly are.

(iv) Fourthly, he maintains that there remains only one alternative—that of taking them as categories of the mind. This analysis of Kant's method also effectively disposes of the contention that his method was much logical and epistemological too. There are all the signs of a practical application of the exclusive type of proof. His characterisation of pure mathematics as a body of synthetic propositions can be questioned and condemned, as has been done by Russell, and the exhaustiveness of the alternatives considered may not be granted.

From where do we get such necessary and universal knowledge? Certainly not from senses; for this knowledge is independent of sense-experience. For Kant all knowledge is in the form of judgements. Genuine knowledge is a necessary and universal judgement. Sensations have nothing as necessary or universal in them. Hence genuine knowledge must be inherent in the very constitution of mind or mind itself, the very essence of mind, the essential fundamental law which determines the manner of all the functions of mind. The mind is not an empty capsule as Locke thought, not a passive recipient of sensations, but a dynamic active agent which modifies the form of the sense-material, gives it a different shape, casts it in the mould of order, unity and method, and reorganises its constitution. So in our knowledge we have material from the senses, unity and order from the mind or understanding. Without sensations or perceptions knowledge is empty; without mind or understanding knowledge is blind. Thus Kant puts his whole problem—How are synthetic judgements *a priori* in mathematics, physics and metaphysics possible? The whole of his 'critique of Pure Reason' is an attempt to answer this question.

Kant observed that sensations by themselves are just subjective states and have to be referred to space and time in order to acquire the character of objectivity in knowledge. Sensations provide matter, while space and time the form. In our process of knowledge we first organise sensations by the application of the perceptual categories of space and time, and then again organise these perceptions by the application of the conceptual categories, the pure concepts and judgments, which are twelve in number. Sensations by themselves cannot give us knowledge; they have to get themselves arranged about an object in space and time, and then we say we have the perception of an object. Without the aid of space and time there can be no perception, for sensations independently give us no knowledge of any object. Space and time are the *a priori* modes or ways of perception, and can also by themselves become contents of pure perception independent of objects. They are *a priori,* because they are the pre-conditions for the formation of sensations into perceptions. And as the laws of mathematics are the laws of space and time, they are *a priori* laws.

According to the empiricists, perceptions are the results of a spontaneous grouping of sensations; but to Kant this is brought about by a purpose that is detectable in the mind itself and in the sensibility of the understanding. Kant rejects the views of Locke and Hume and concludes that the understanding plays an important role in the formation of perceptive judgements. Yet, perceptive judgements, which by nature are distinct and separated, cannot give us real knowledge. As the reformulation of sensations into perceptions is done by the application of perceptual categories of space and time, similarly the perceptions are transformed into conceptive judgements by the application of conceptual categories of the understanding. Besides as the sensations are grouped, arranged and united about objects in perception by means of the *a priori* laws of space and time; so perceptions are connected, related and organised by conceptions about the ideas of the categories of quantity, quality, relation and modality. The perceptions are cast in the moulds of these categories of the understanding and transformed into concepts and judgments. This becomes possible on account of the presence of an unifying consciousness or synthetic unity of apperception in us. The function as well as the essence of the understanding is in this arrangement and organisation of sensations and perceptions. The connecting link between percepts and concepts is the time-form, which Kant calls the *'transcendental schema'*. This order and unity in sensations and perceptions is brought about by these laws which are inherent in the understanding or the mind itself. Kant recognises that the *things-in-themselves* cannot be the causes of this organised character seen in knowledge, for we affirm their existence only by inference from the scattered sensations that we receive from outside. Thus the capacity for order and unity has to be attributed to the mind or the understanding alone. The differences that are observed in the degree of knowledge possessed by different persons prove that order is brought into sensations not by the sensations themselves but by the *a priori* laws of the mind, which is an active judge as well as law giver and a wax pond just receiving impressions. The laws and the ordered unity of the world are therefore the laws and the ordered unity of the categories of the mind. What we call things are not *things-in-themselves,* but the categories of the mind alone, objectified in space and time. That means, we see in things only the necessary and universal laws of the mind that recognise themselves in the objects of the world. Kant has tried to save the world of physics, as he had tried to save mathematics.

Therefore according to Kant's explanation sensible objects are derived from a substratum of intelligible objects that exist independent of our experience of them. *Things-in-themselves* are objects without a subject, beyond space and time, separate from a perceiving subject. An appearance must be recognised as already indicating a relation to something in itself, i.e., an object independent of sensibility. So, Kant vehemently rejected the subjective idealism of George Berkeley, since the inner subjectivity of the mind is as much of an appearance or representation as external objects. *Things-in-themselves* are the metaphysical ground of both external and internal phenomena. Therefore these *things-in-themselves* transcend the perceptual and conceptual categories of the mind, which are valid for explaining only the finite world. What objects may be in themselves, would never become known to us even through the most enlightened knowledge. The transcendental object, which is the cause of appearance . . . can be thought neither as quality or quantity nor as reality or as substance. Human understanding cannot know these Noumena through any of the categories, and that it must therefore think them only under the title of an unknown something.

The Sanatana doctrine never accepts *things-in-themselves* but states that the ultimate reality, which is the substratum of the phenomenal world, is the supporting causal foundation of the world; it can be labelled as ***"thing-in-itself"***. For, it is the formless, partless, infinite, unconditioned ground of all relations. The Absolute Self is the archetype which illumines the intellect engendering the reflected individual Self and the world. The reflected image is falsely mistaken for the archetype, until the ignorance is negated; and there the reflection discontinues, and only the Pure Self remains. When one single '*thing in itself*' can be the supporting ground of all phenomena, it is useless to imagine '*things-in-themselves.*' Since the mental world is also a part of the ignorance. Perceptual awareness reveals what exists, but does not subjectively create external objects out of itself. An inseparable association between the subject and the object does not mean that they are identical. Since we experience an object as an external entity and distinguish between the subject and the object, this world exists separately from our perception of it. The waking state unlike the dream experience, is derived from sense perception rather than memory, is public not private, persists in a coherent manner for a long time and is not negated by our waking consciousness. For such experiential perceptions only one single '*thing-in-itself*' can be the supporting causal foundation without any difficulty. That *'thing-in-itself'* is the ultimate reality, the Absolute Self, which cannot be known by discursive reason. Pure reality, absolute self, which cannot be known by discursive reason, thus, belongs to no genius, it possesses no qualities, being actionless it cannot be indicated by any act or by a word implying an act, it being not related to anything else. You cannot perceive that which pervades knowledge. Hence Absolute Pure Self cannot be known by intellect or denoted by words which can signify only a category of a thing. So ultimately we can say that Kant's world of *things-in-themselves* is a needless superfluity.

Kant, according to the Sanatana view, is not correct in supposing that the logical categories of the human mind can modify or affect the constitution of our knowledge, that we know only the logical categories and that what we call physical objects are only the objectifications of these categories of Human mind. The German Philosopher Johanne Fichte, Kant's pupil, rejected his teacher's division of the world into objective and subjective parts and had developed an idealistic philosophy that also had great influence in the 19th century on the socialists. Indeed, if a philosophy is to be judged by or along with its logical outcome then the philosophy of Kant is to be judged by that of Hegel and Fichte.

The German Philosopher **Johanne Fichte,** Kant's pupil, maintained that philosophy must be a science; it must be developed systematically from a single self-evident proposition, and it must make clear the ground of all experiences. Thus he took exception to Kant's theory of the unknowable **'things-in-themselves'** and also to his dichotomy between speculative and practical reason.

The true Sanatana method holds that the physical world is either the manifestation of God (Empirical stand point) or the super-imposition on the pure self by ignorance (Absolute stand point), and that the existence of objects is independent of human thinking and of its logical laws, though the human mind contributes much in determining the value of the objects by projecting on them its own desires, feelings and emotions. It may be true that certain desires, feelings and emotions are common to all mankind, yet this universality of certain psychological conditions cannot be made a factor that can affect the existence of the physical objects. Logic too is not the same as metaphysics, if by logic we mean the laws of mere human reasoning and thinking. Because Human thinking is not a part of reality in the sense of cosmic existence. Only the cosmic mind or will of God can have such reality and only the logic of such God's cosmic mind can be identical with the laws of a metaphysics of reality. And also it is only this cosmic mind that can modify the nature of the objects of knowledge by the categories or laws of its constitution. In the Sanatana method world is ideal in the sense that it is in the idea of God, but not in the idea of man or even in the ideas of all men. Again, space and time as well as the physicality and externality of the objects of the universe cannot be considered to be realities from the point of view of God, for He is a Spiritual Being, and the appearances of these, therefore, are to be understood as the necessary counterparts of the notion of our individual existence. The physical world has an existence totally independent of human thinking or willing, but it becomes dependent on the thinking and willing of the individual only when the human mind rises above itself and gets unified with the mind of God. Thus the world exists only so long as human individuality persists, and not when it is transcended into the cosmic mind. We can express this as follows—As long as an individual exists, other individuals too exist, which are as much real as itself, and there is a physical world which is also as much real as all the individuals, and so not dependent on their thoughts or laws of thinking. As long as this state of affairs continues, we have to accept the existence of a cosmic mind and God which is the generator, controller as well as destroyer of this physical world and of all the individuals in it. It is that cosmic mind which completely determines the nature of the world and its laws. This independence of the physical world over individuals and its thoughts, and also the existence of the cosmic mind or God are necessary and unavoidable facts implied by the individualistic experience. But when the individual mind is transcended to the state of cosmic mind, there will be neither the individual nor the world; there will be the absolute-experience only. Ultimately the world discloses its spiritual being. This explains in what way the world is independent or has extrâmental reality, in what way ideal or purely dependent on mind, in what way relative to the interaction of subject and object and in what way non-existent. This is the glory of the Sanatana tradition.

Kant recognises that though mathematics and the physical sciences are in conformity with the universal laws of thought and the system of logic, and so necessary and valid for every mind, this necessity and validity of theirs is limited to phenomena, and so they are relative. The world of sense experience is an appearance; it does not consist of *things-in-themselves,* for they cannot be known, though they lie as the background of all phenomena. Some interpreters of Kant object to his assertion of the *things-in themselves* as dogmatic, for, when they cannot be known at all, as Kant says, how can their existence be asserted that they exist? Thus the critics think that this is an unwarranted assumption contrary to Kant's theory that nothing that is known is more than an appearence. Even the *things-in-themselves* ought to be restricted to the categories of the mind, for it is the mind that asserts their existence. Others try to save Kant from this charge by holding that this concept of *things-in-themselves* does not make them known as realities, but it is only a limiting concept which Kant has no objection to include within phenomena, because the aim of this concept is only to point out the limits of possible knowledge or experience. But the Sanatana tradition would go ahead of Kant, as well as his critics and supporters, and suggest to Kant himself that the *things-in-themselves* are not mere postulates or hypothetical suppositions as he thinks, neither phenomena of the finite categories nor even just limiting concepts, but intimation of a super-mental reality, which Kant posited, even without his own knowing, through shades of a supersensuous intuition, and which he, by analogy from physical objects of perception, wrongly supposed to be many in number. Really there is one *"Thing-in-itself"* and not many *"Things-in-Themselves"*. Sometimes Kant even gives a hint that *things-in-themselves* are material objects, though their exact nature cannot be known by us, which would obviously be a lapse into the Lockian theory of representationism. How can we say that the objects are material when they are not known? Kant cannot make himself consistent unless he admits the *thing-in-itself* to an Eternal Spiritual Being, indivisible, and so infinite or non-dual.

Now Kant, with his theory of the categories and by limiting all knowledge to appearances, tries to give a death blow to metaphysics, declaring with a hardened intellect that not only our knowledge of the objects of the world, but also our knowledge of Empirical Soul and God is an appearance, a phenomenon of the categories of the intellect and the mind. Metaphysical knowledge, as per Kant, is limited to phenomena, there is no metaphysics of "Being as Being" or of the "that which is". All such metaphysics is involved in antinomies and paralogisms. Kant shows that we can prove that the world has a beginning in time and also that it has no beginning in time; that a compound substance consists of simple parts and also does not consist of simple parts; that there is freedom and also that all things are determined, thus no freedom; that there is an absolutely necessary being and also there is no such being. Because reason cannot establish ultimate truths. We are caught in the grips of phenomenal experience from which we cannot extricate ourselves. Kant's this statement is similar to the "Syadavada theory" of the Jainism, in the East. As the Jains say—we can say a thing is; we can say it is not; we can say it is and it is not-both; we cannot say that a thing is; we cannot say it is not; we cannot say it is and it is not-both; we cannot say anything about anything. Such statements are self-devastating. As this can be applied to Kant himself and his philosophy stating as follows—Kant had taken birth in time and also not in time; He had limbs, organs etc..., and also he did not have any limb, organs etc.; he was a man and also he was not a man; etc. Then we can say that Kant was a great literate intellectual fool who befooled the whole world, for, he could not even make himself consistent about his own existence and his thoughts.

But still, the greatness of Kant lies in that he has thoroughly investigated and grasped the powers and limits of reason, and knows to what extent reason can provide man with genuine knowledge. But his weakness is in that he stretches the function of reason beyond their limits, to a province over which reason cannot have sway, ending in a bitter decision that the *things-in-themselves* cannot be known or experienced and also foolishly tried to construct a metaphysics of reality. Thus if Hume gives us scepticism, Kant gives agnosticism. Both leave us in the same position as far as our knowledge of reality is concerned. Kant did not notice that his antinomies are not real contradictions but different perspectives, different views of reality, all true at some time, at a particular stage in the development of the powers of our knowledge. Kant himself knows that the predicament in which we are landed by the antinomies is due to our falsely supposing that space, time and cause are external and independent of perception. When these forms of perception get identified with knowledge itself, in a manner different from that in which Kant's categories are contained in the understanding, all these antinomies get resolved in the wholesome of perception which is super-sensuous intuition. As it has been already shown that the world is real for purposes of certain aspects of life, ideal for certain others, relative at some stage, and non-existent at another. These are not contradictions, but piecemeal views of reality given to the mind which cannot know it as a whole at one stroke. It may appear from an exclusively abstract point of view of the pure reason that our knowledge of reality is phenomenal, but we should say that this is merely an act of super errogation on the part of reason, and untenable thesis. The effect cannot know its cause without it ceasing to be an effect. It is futile to know reality, as such, through the mind or the reason. Kant admitted this for a reason totally different from the one which the Sanatana method gives. Kant limits experience to sense, mind, understanding and reason, without caring to head their presuppositions; so he denies the possibility of a genuine metaphysics of reality. But to us, experience does not consist of merely these (senses, mind, intellect and reason); there is another faculty of knowledge on which these are based and without which these are meaningless, and which is in a position to build a sound metaphysics, comprehensive and satisfactory. This basis, this presupposition of all relative knowledge, is the Soul, the Pure Self, the arguer, the doubter, the ground lying behind scepticism, phenomenalism, agnosticism and for all other isms; which is not a matter of doubt, not an appearance and not unknown too.

Free Will and Necessity

Some doubt that if pure consciousness is the only reality and if God is the Universal Being then the freedom of the empirical soul, i.e., the individual, can only be conditional, and not absolute. Freedom of choice in the individual is relegated to the experiences of the appearances that constitute the world, and effort becomes a process of the transmission of the impetus of universal activity done by an universal ego through an individual ego. The force of the universe, as the will of God, causes an all-round evolution of things in space and time. As the universal will is supreme, it may be said that there is an external determinism of the scheme of creation, preservation and destruction. But this universal will acts not merely in the objective physical universe, but also in the subjective mental states. When the mind is endowed with the consciousness of personality and individuality, it recceives the vibration of the cosmic will through the medium of the constituents of its personality. The light that passes through a coloured glass seems to acquire the colour of that glass. The unique nature of the individual is self-centredness. Limitation of body, desire for objects, and intense self-respect, etc. are certain traits of this notable state. The universal will, when it passes through the prism of individuality, appears to imbibe these strange attributes which the mind arrogates to itself, of its own accord. In this process, the mind, instead of realising that the impulse for activity which it feels within itself is but the ingress of the universal into its individual processes, commits an error in yielding to the dictates of the individual ego and assuming for itself the role of a real agent, a doer and an enjoyer. When this impulse is deliberately associated with the personal ego, it goes by the name of the effort actuated by a felt free will. Thus it becomes clear that free-will and effort are names given to the manner in which the cosmic will is erroneously received through the medium of the personal ego and attributed to it as a reality.

The answer to this doubt is as follows—Effort, however, can be actually directed according to one's own will, as it is actually done by all spiritual aspirants, when it is illuminated by the light of the higher understanding. When the whole personality is lighted up by the higher knowledge, the personal ego begins to act by accepting its guidance. Here comes about the peculiar joint action of the personal ego, which assumes the role of agency, and the superior knowledge, which directs the individual beyond itself. As far as effort, as such, is concerned, it is to be considered as a result of mistaking the action of the universal impetus for individual power, but, when this effort moves in the direction of contemplation on the Divine Being, it becomes a process of self-purification and spiritual enlightenment. All other forms of effort are misdirected in different degrees, and lead to bondage and pain. Ultimately, We have to distinguish between the lower effort of the ignorant individual and the higher one of the wise spiritual aspirant. The higher effort causes in the end a cessation of all personal initiative in the experience of Reality. Rightly directed effort aims at liberating the individual gradually from the false notion of its being an independent agent in the performance of actions. The solution to the problem of the relation of free will and necessity lies in our recognising that the individual freedom is nothing but experiencing the way in which the absolute consciousness is envisaged by temporal processesss as a scenario depicted on one's self.

The question of the freedom of the Soul is an agelong one. In the words of James Jeans in his *physics and philosophy* (pp. 206) states as follows—"Spinoza thought that our actions and experiences are in actual fact determined by a sort of mathematical necessity, like that of a wheel in a machine, but that we feel ourselves free if we enjoy doing what actually we are doing under compulsion; a stone in the air would think itself free if it could forget the hand that had thrown it. Or, to take a more homely illustration which is not Spinoza's, I know that I choose Jam roll because I like it and I feel myself free in choosing because I do not stop to think that my liking is the inevitable result of my inheritance and upbringing, of the present state of my health and of my sugar metabolism, and of all sorts of things which is quite beyond my power to change at the moment. Hegel, and at a later period, Alexander, held very similar options. Kant thought that we feel ourselves free in just so far as our actions appear rational to us; if I rationally run downstairs to welcome a friend, my action seems free to me; but if I run downstairs because I am afraid of a ghost, it will seem to me that I acted under compulsion".

So according to the above statement, it is the condition of the mind that finally determines whether an action is done with freedom of will or under the stress of necessity and force. Freedom in this world is really the individual's consciousness identified with a particular action or group of actions under consideration, with an unconsciousness of the fact that these actions are but bits of the process of the universe directed by the laws of the Absolute. When the impersonal law gets translated in terms of a conscious individuality which is inseparable from a sense of personal agency, it goes by the name of free will and self-effort.

What we call our freedom is, according to Plotinus, simply the power of obeying our true and essential nature. True freedom does not belong to the appetitive side of human nature, to our desires or to our passions, it is not even a property of mind, ego, intellect or senses, for, it is seen that these impulses restrict the freedom of man in acting otherwise than as they direct. Plotinus holds that complete freedom is not given to us as long as our desires are prompted by finite needs. The connection of our conscious with the material body makes us dependent on the general laws of the physical world, over which we, as individuals, have no control. The individual is a complex structure, it partakes of elements that are subjected to necessity and also a principle whose essential nature is freedom. We may be individuals and as such under compulsion to obey Nature (the universal ego's will); but we are also, as persons, each of us a whole. Though as parts we are all determined, yet as wholes we are free. The highest freedom belongs to the Absolute, and we are ultimately not different from it, and thus enjoy freedom in the real sense. The whole is present in every part, and the part is free to the extent to which the whole is manifested in it. "We are, therefore, not merely cogs in a great machine; we are the machine itself, and the mind which directs it". The soul which has perfectly realised its inner essential nature is perfectly free. "The imperfect man is pulled and pushed by forces which are external to himself, just because he is himself still external to his true being". Though the law of cause and effect operates everywhere inviolably and determines the movement of everything, we as self-conscious spirits are "ourselves causative principles". The principle of freedom in us is in the innermost spirit that we all are, for the Spirit cannot be determined by any cause outside itself. Freedom is—"the will of the Higher Soul to return to its own principle. The element of freedom in our practical activities in this underlying motive, the spiritual activity of the Soul". When the individual experiences enlightenment, it will enjoy freedom. The will then becomes a good will, and the attainment of its desire is tantamount to spiritual perception, the perception of the glory of the spirit which is absolutely free. Freedom is the principle of abiding by the laws of the Absolute, which is our Self. (Vide, *W.R. Inge, The Philosophy of Plotinus*).

The freedom that the ordinary man speaks of is an apparent freedom to will certain things and to act in certain ways, but he does not consider whether he has freedom to will, or whether he has knowledge as to why he should will in a particular manner at all. That a man thinks he is free cannot be accepted as a proof that he is really free, for it has been observed that a subject under hypnosis carries out a train of activity, suggested to him under hypnosis, and, after awakening from the hypnotic state, gives reasons of his own when asked to explain why he acted in that way. Since the hypnotist knows the real reason behind the subject's actions, and since this motive or reason differs from the one which the subject offers, it has been suggested that the reasons for our actions can be different from what we believe them to be, and that this indicates the existence and operation of unknown forces. We feel we are free because we are aware only of our present volitions and not of their real causes. It is our limitation to self-consciousness that makes us feel that we are free. This has led psychologists to throw overboard free-will altogether, and assume an unconscious realm of the psyche as the sole determinant of all conscious behaviour. Our thoughts and desires are said to be expressions of the unconscious, only certain aspects of which are allowed to enter the surface of consciousness. The so-called freedom of the individual is thus threatened by the control which the unconscious impulses have on the conscious life of man. According to C.E.M. Joad—"If, in short, consciousness is rightly regarded as a by-product of the unconsciousness processes, it is clearly determined by the processes which produce it. Conscious events are merely the smoke and flame given off by the workings of the subterranean psychological machinery of which we all are unconscious." Therefore the instincts and impulses are held by psycho-analysts to be the main-spring of all individual action. Even the unselfish actions or desireless activities of man are supposed to be driven by instincts over which he has no control, and of which he has no knowledge. Even the intellect is dubbed as a mere rationalisation of inner urges. Intellectual activity and ratiocinative processes are classed as operations of irrational instincts in the plane of objective consciousness. Human life is therefore depicted as a striving of the impulses to seek satisfaction in the achievement of their particular ends. These findings of depth-psychology, have, no doubt an element of truth in them; but they do not give us the whole truth. This will be, discussed in detail in Appendix No. 1 while taking up a critical analysis over Kant's lecture on freedom as enlightenment.

The ideas of freedom and necessity, of the nature of causality and of a necessary Being above the world, of an ultimate causeless cause, etc.; which for Kant are not above the phenomena of the categories of the understanding, thus, hinge upon the problem of Self, of an immutable, incorruptible, immortal, simple, indivisible, spiritual substance or Being. For Kant, such a Self is not only inconceivable but unknowable too; our concept of it is, for him, involved in phenomena. So it is not above the finitising categories, hence the concept of the world and God, too, which bear relations to the Self, are phenomenal. Kant says that we know ourselves not as we are but as we appear to ourselves through the categories. We know the world not as it is but as it appears to us through the categories. We know God not as He is, but as He passes through our understanding and reason. Thus the world as such, Soul and God are all *things-in-themselves* and so exist beyond experience.

We cannot, however, charge Kant with the guilt of denying Soul, world and God altogether; for what he seems to say is that these cannot be known through sensation, perception, understanding or reason; else there would be no meaning in positing the *things-in-themselves* by him. But the trouble with him is that he could not accept that we have any other kind of experience other than the sensuous, the mental and the intellectual. He has, no doubt, the genius to conceive an intellectual intuition which, he says, if we could possess it, would enable to see things face to face, in their true essence. But he denies its reality and accepts it only as a probability and says we have only sensuous intuition, but know nothing as supersensuous. He denies an immediate integral intuition of even our own selves and makes the Self, just an object of the discursive reason. His opinion is that one knows oneself but not one's Self. He smacks of Hume when he says that-what we know of ourselves are only successive mental states, percepts, and nothing more. We have only a thought of Self, not a perception of Self, and this thought is a bundle of such states. Kant wavers between this view and the one that radically differentiates him from Hume, the admission of a synthetic or transcendental unity of apperception, a unifying ego, an I, which cannot be identified with a perception or a thought, and without which no knowledge is possible. But this ego of Kant is different from the Pure Real Self of the Sanatana method, for the former is still an empirical form relating itself to the empirical experiences. Kant holds that his ego transcends empirical consciousness; but really it cannot do so, for it becomes according to him an individualised will which ever presses beyond itself. But he distinguishes it from the empirical ego as the Sanatana method separates the Pure Self from the Empirical Self. The notion of the Self appears to Kant to be an object of the discursive reason because he deliberately makes it an object of the reason. We do not know our own existence through the reason, but we have an immediate integral apprehension of our Self being identical with an indivisible consciousness. This fact is too clear but requires extra contemplation over it. Our Conscious Being never becomes an object; it ever persists in being the ground and presupposition of all our processes of knowledge. If the Self is to become an object, where will the knowledge of this object subsist? This knowledge would require another Self to base itself; and this process of reasoning would end in an infinite regress. Actually the apprehension of the Self does not admit of any relations, any process of knowing, any kind of duality in regard to itself. The Sanatana method declares that there are certain spiritual laws which we daily experience in our own selves, though indistinctly on account of the presence of a veil of ignorance covering the Self, and which exist even prior to the categories of the understanding, we are not able to conceive them directly by our supersensous intuitive power. As Kant's *a priori* categories or principles of knowledge are universal and determine the nature of perceptions and things, so the Sanatana method too holds that there are principles of knowledge which are more universal and necessary than Kant's judgements and categories, which even determine these judgements and categories. Knowledge through the understanding is by no means the only possible one. There is a spiritual realisation of the Absolute, which is not only a mere probability but also a certainty, a certainty greater than that offered by the fact of our experience of an empirical world of things.

Thus Kant is a person who knows, and yet knows not that he knows it. He makes suggestive statements, comes to the very borderland of Reality, but stops there. This he does because he is unable to step beyond the realm of the understanding and finds himself hemmed in from all sides by the laws of understanding. He says that the concepts or the ideas of the pure reason, the ideas of a unified world, Soul and God, are merely regulative principles which reveal the limits of possible knowledge and asserts that there is a transcendental reality beyond our possible experience. Now, it is here that, Kant does not know that his assertion of a transcendental reality is imposible merely with the aid of his categories. He owed the possibility of this concept of things-in-themselves to a touch of the supersensuous intuition, though this type of intuition never came to him as a direct experience or direct perception. He says that the things-in-themselves can be thought of, and not known. Now question arises How does thought function? It does through the categories: Can we apply the categories in our thinking of *things-in-themselves*? No. Then by what means Kant thinks about them? He cannot say that—I think about them through reason and not the mind that thinks them, for even the reason functions through the categories. It is obvious then that he thinks them with a faculty transcending the senses and the categories. And this is nothing but the supersensuous intuition.

Kant overlooks the fact that the reason always exhibits an irresistible confidence in its powers to apprehend the things-in-themselves in empirical perception. It refuses to yield to the threats of the understanding that what it knows are mere projections of the relative categories of possible knowledge. It is impossible to disregard the superhuman urge within us which is ever anxious to recognise the supreme need for the indivisible, the infinite, the real in us and in all things. Kant also forgets that he cannot account for the correspondence of the forms of the categories of the mind with the material of sense-perception outside, unless there is a common conscious background, a unity underlying the two. Knowledge is possible because of an existence which is common to both the subject and the object. If the categories of the understanding do not bear a consciousness-relation to the material supplied by the senses, there would be no adaptation of the former to the latter. The relation between the mind within and the objects outside is a knowledge-relation, and knowledge or consciousness should be an underlying unity covering both the knower and the known. In other words knowledge conceived as the pre-supposition and ground of all possible human knowledge in empirical experience is universal existence itself. It is this independent, omnipresent existence-consciousness that we term 'The Absolute' in Sanatana method.

If as Kant thinks, the ideas of reason have merely a regulative use, valid only until they give a unity and order to our knowledge, and if we are to act merely as if their objects existed, then we would be living in a world of imaginations, illusions nay, life would be impossible. The meaning that we instinctively discover in life detests any such propositions, and affirms a preciousity and value in existence that cannot be compared with anything we perceive in the world of sense. The ideas of reason are not mere probabilities or future possibilities, but stand for an eternal fact that is the very basis of the entire structure of possible knowledge here. The possibility of having in our reason such ideas arises not, as Kant thinks, on account of reason's abstracting the conditions from the conditioned, but by the very pre-suppositions made by the reason itself. We proceed not from the conditioned to the unconditioned, but from the un-conditioned to the conditioned. We begin with a self-evident unconditioned consciousness which is in us and without assuming which, as a fact there can be no thought or life. Even the functions of the ideas of reason as the pointers to the limits of experience imply the existence of the limitless, for a knowledge of what is beyond limits is at once included in our knowledge of limits. A criticism of epistemology is demanded today, of the very subject that emerged as the criticism of the logical or dogmatic procedure of reason. The doctrine of truth and error, if it could be systematised according to a principle, would furnish such a criticism of criticism. The two degrees of criticism are not distinguished and there is so far no principle on which we may decide between rival epistemologies. In the Kantian Critiques, there is the hint of a transcendental psychology behind the general theory of knowledge, with an occasional recognition of the necessity of distinguishing between them. Kant speaks, for example, of error being due to the 'subjective use' of reason as distinct from its intrinsically logical function and of certain principles being real to reason as employed in an extra-theoretic 'interest'. His theory of knowledge is properly concerned with the general logical function which is common to true knowing and error. His references to reason as a subjective faculty capable of perverse or extra-logical use are accordingly to be looked upon as mere *obliterdicta* within his epistomology and as really belonging to transcendental psychology which was always assumed but never sufficiently distinguished by him.

The systematic doctrine of truth and error would be the same as or a part of his transcendented psychology. To empirical psychology, the logical function going astray and yielding a false content conveys no meaning at all. Logic can recognise error only as a blind fact and epistemology should regard it as a miracle: the question of explaining its possibility does not arise at all in these subjects. Yet a theory of truth and error is ordinarily claimed to be established by a conscious or self-conscious logical method and there is no recognition so far as any mystery of cognitive level about it. One tendency however is noticeable in theories thus established—viz., to slur over the absolute distinction that is recognised in common sense between truth and error. The suggestion is put forward in different forms that error is a partial truth, truth within a limited extent and context; and it is sometimes proposed in a manner to drop the conception of truth itself, a content being taken to be true only in the sense that is known or 'asserted'. Such flagrant opposition to common sense requires to be justified by something more than the consideration that it is conceivable and logically irrefutable. It is necessary to show on the one hand that a doctrine of this kind is itself knowledge and a mere hypothesis and on the other that a theory admitting the absolute distinction of truth and error cannot be maintained. Descartes was confident that we cannot know ourselves as finite beings without referring this knowledge of ours to the existence of the infinite. Further, how can the conditioned ideas which we have been given by the conceptual categories give rise to the ideas of the infinite, the unconditioned, the immortal? How can the idea of the Absolute arise in us if it is not inherent already in our own consciousness? How can even an idea or a notion or a concept of the Absolute or the infinite become possible if our consciousness is completely locked within and bound by the finite categories? Kant misses to discover in the ideas of reason real *a priori* principles which logically precede the categories of the understanding.

H.J. Paton, a well known Kantian scholar, tells us that Kant does not really seem to have argued from the existence of the given in experience to the *things-in-themselves* as its cause, but rather seemed to regard them as immediately present to us in all our experiences. A knowledge that the world is phenomenal is based on an inner conviction, pointing not merely to a probability or a possibility but to the pure reality of all empirical realities, and suggesting that an immutable Being exists transcending the phenomena. It is Kant's intellectual bias that prevents him from accepting these truths which shine before us like the sun in daylight. To the senses the real, no doubt, appears as an abstract idea, for it is far removed from the reach of their knowledge. Kant shows a prejudice in favour of the sole authority of sense-knowledge when he disregards the claims of the ideas of reason and relegates them to the limb of probabilities. The organising capacity, the law and order and the passion for unity present in the mind prove the existence of a unitary and indivisible conscious Self. Space and time though empirically real, are transcendentally ideal, and the necessity as well as universality of the truths of mathematics which is possible only in spatial extension and the time-form felt as a succession of homogeneous moments, and of physics which owes allegiance to the laws of mathematics in conformity with the categories of the understanding, which finally emerges out of the mind as an outward phenomenal expression of the unity underlying the processes of all our knowledge. The immediate consciousness of Self requires it to be recognised as unlimited, pervading all phenomena. This consciousness in it is the Supreme Non-dual Being. It is God in Sanatana method when viewed in relation to the world of experience; it is Absolute Existence-Consciousness-Bliss in its own being. As the categories of the understanding suit to the sense-material in giving us knowledge, the ideas of reason refer to ultimate reality, though we require a deeper insight to appreciate this fact. And even as the categories by themselves have no significance in knowledge without their adaptation to sense-material received in empirical perception, the ideas of reason also have no significance of their own in knowledge if they do not agree to the Reality experienced in super-sensuous intuition. These ideas do not merely constitute a regulative method in life, but act as representations of the Reality existing by its own right. The systematic unity which the idea of the Supreme Being gives to life is the shadow cast by the existence of the Supreme Being.

Kant's argument against the ontological proof for the existence of God too needs correction. His illustration that the idea of my having some thalers in my pocket book does not prove that they exist there, is not applicable to the concept of God in Sanatana method. What Kant is to be taught is that he could not have the idea of thalers, if thalers did not have existence. What is important is not that whether they exist in the pocket book or elsewhere, but that they exist; their existence or non-existence in the pocket book is irrelevant to the question of the idea of God, for the idea of God is the idea of the omnipresent, the infinite and not about something which exists somewhere localised as in the pocket book or outside it, and so much an idea should imply the existence of what it points to, even as the idea of thalers proves that thalers do exist. The reason why Kant finds himself obliged to deny existence of God from the idea of God is that he entirely cuts off thought from Reality, while in fact, thought at one stage of its being gets identified with Reality. The cosmological argument for the existence of God depends on the ontological argument, and gets explained together with it. The contingent demands a cause, that is non-contingent and non-accidental, which is necessary to give completeness and a systematic character to experience. That such a cause does not exist cannot follow from the contingent nature of phenomena; on the other hand, contingent phenomena affirm an absolute ground. We are bound to admit the existence of an Intelligent Being on which phenomena depend. In his (Kant's) account of the physio-theological proof for the existence of God. He (Kant) makes God an architect of the world building upon a hampering material, but does not think that God can be shown to be the creator of the world, subjecting the world to his will. It is a false abstraction of the idea of God from the nature of things that is responsible for Kant's supposition that God is an outward agency working on a given material. The idea of God includes the ideas of omnipresence, eternity and infinity, which forbid any attempt to exclude God's presence from the world. God can have meaning only when He comprehends the world on the very existence of His consciousness, which not only takes Him beyond even creatorship but also makes Him the absolute-existence. In Sanatana method the Absolute is the only reality, which includes and transcends every form of experience. This Absolute is the Existence-Consciousness-Bliss in its pure and totally real form.

Moreover whatever Kant speaks is deeply rooted in his erroneous reasoning. There is no reason in this world which is perfect and absolute. Because reason has its own limitations; it cannot trespass everything, every experience or other proofs and give us a perfect knowledge of anything.

The Limitations of Reason

The true nature of God and His creation cannot be intellectually comprehended, for logic is a proud child of the dualist prejudice. If God alone is all in this world, the relation between Him and the world, no mortal can hope to know. Man's idea of God is highly defective, for God, as man understands Him, is relative to the appearance of the world. God is a pure subject opposed to a world of creation set before him, as an object cannot be absolute; and if He is not thus opposed, He ceases to have any external relation to the world. If God is a universal consciousness having the universe as His object, He cannot be connected with it except by a spatio-temporal knowledge. Such a knowing process, however, is inadmissible in the case of God, for He is and should be untouched by the vitiating divisions of space and time. If not so, then there would be no difference between the God and Individual. If not so, then there would be no difference between God and Individual. But without this division, God cannot be distinguished from the Absolute which will not brook any type of objectivation of itself. Even in Sankhian Philosophy of the East, the infinite Soul and insentient root cause which lies with the former in almost every respect in an instance of the defeat which the human intellect has to suffer when it attempts to visualise a reality which is non-mediately related to the universe and yet is not the same as the universe. The God who is in man's mind cannot be freed from the difficulty of having to melt down to indifferentiated Being when His relation to the world is closely examined. God's existence happens to be relative to the demands of His self-manifesting work. He is, as long as the universe is.

Besides, we cannot say that God created the world at any period of time. If the creative act is not in time, it (creative act) being the condition even of time, there would be no creation of a temporal world. Creation is a process, and all process is in time. There is no process that can be dovetailed with eternity. To cause anything, God will have to descend into time, and a descent into time is a descent into finitude, change and a veritable self-destruction. If God is to bear any relation to phenomena, He has to shed His eternal nature first. But somehow He creates and sustains the world without losing His eternality. This the human intellect cannot understand. The Absolute sports in the relative. The individuals of the world arise as appearances participating in a relative interdependence of existence and nature. If there is no child, there is no parent, too. God becomes an object of the notion of the Empirical Self, and a subject with the world as a predicate attached to it.

The logical character of truth and reality attributed to God does not look consistent with our ascribing to Him the ethical character of goodness, the aesthetic character of beauty and the religious character of grace; all of which carry an individualistic purport. If God is the all, such values turn to be different from what they mean to us here in this world. Why has God created the world? It cannot be for his satisfaction, for he has no wish or desire to fulfil. It cannot be with a view of dispensing justice or showing mercy to others, for there are no others, as all beings are subsequent to the creative act. It cannot be a play of God; for play is normally supposed to be the result of a need felt within to direct outside the excess of energy in the psycho-physical organism, to overcome fatigue or boredom, or to replenish the system with fresh energy after an exhausting work. If God is only a witness of the sports of the root cause of the world which moves and acts at the inspiration received from His mere existence, He would have a determining element outside Him, which would prevent Him from being an absolute monarch. God is the pure self envisaged by our experiential conditions in relation to a world of change. The question of creation is restricted to the world of the senses and the intellect, thus the answer to it cannot but be empirically bound. There cannot be a correct answer to an erroneous question. That the world is, is a belief of ours, and the whole problem of creation hinges on how we react to our environment as dismembered bodies in a cosmic society.

Kant has clearly denied the mystical presence of the divine in humans. Religious experience which is based on feeling and not reason which can lead to fanaticism and superstition. Super conscious intellectual intuition of God or the soul is not at all possible for humans, who cannot penetrate beyond the phenomenal representation.

As per Sanatana view, it is possible to have a mystical transcendental experience of God, the ultimate reality. The sages had achieved spiritual illumination and created a practical religious philosophy that focusses on attaining super-sensuous super-conscious transcendental consciousness. So they declared—"Know thy soul, transcend all sorrows, and reach the eternal fountain of eternal joy. Be illumined by this knowledge, and you have nothing to fear." "The ego has disappeared. I have realised my identity with the Pure Ultimate Reality. I know nothing but joy, limitlessness, unbounded, etc. . ." He who knows the soul is free from every kind of bondage. He is full of glory, He is the greatest of the great . . . He tastes the sweet, unending bliss of the Soul and is satisfied."

The futility of the logical methods in determining the nature of God does not imply, however, that there is no intelligence underlying the world and influencing it throughout. For the denial of such a Being would entail a denial of the world, and consequently, our ownselves as individuals. Certain inherent-defects in our faculties of knowing prevent us from comprehending transcendent truths in a proper manner. It does not follow that the invisible has always non-existed. If we are, the world is, and if the world is, then God also is. If God is not, the world also is not; and we as individuals, too, cannot be. There is reciprocal dependence of the existence of these three principles always. Our concepts are always relative. The absolutely real is only the Pure Self. But as long as we accept our own existence as diversified elements in the world, then a sovereign being giving meaning to life cannot be doubtful. Our own conscious powers within us urge us to accept that God is. The scriptures corroborate our inner spiritual aspirations and extol God who is the creator-operator and destroyer of this world. It is the nature of God to create, to manifest and unfold the world; there is no other reason for it that is humanly conceivable. To show that God has no personal interest whatsoever, it is also shown that He only helps creation, which is really a manifestation or expression of the dormant potencies of the individuals who, not being liberated at the end of the previous cycle, existed in a latent form during the dissolution of the universe after that cycle. Just like rain helps the growth of the plant but the nature of the plant depends on the nature of the seed from which it grows. In this case the world is a cycle of creation, preservance and destruction. Such cycles are beginningless and endless.

Strictly speaking the truth, the theory of creation of the world by God, God Himself and the individuals, is not to be taken as a statement of ultimate fact; but is meant to serve as a working hypothesis introduced to bring out the idea of the non-difference of the God, world and individuals from the Pure Self. Thus creation or entrance of God into the world by His immanence, are eulogical concepts intended to bring home to the mind of man the fact of the secondlessness of Self and the total dependence of the world on Self. No explanation of the, why or how, of creation, and no concept of God as the supreme ruler of the world, can be finally satisfactory; for such statements and concepts are based on a false faith in the individuality of the Self and the variety of the world of experience. But they are serviceable as a *modus operandi* in directing the individual from his ignorant prejudices of a bodily existence to the splendour of the Absolute. The Absolute Pure Self is not in need of knowing itself either as a subject or an object. But it has somehow to be related to the world until we as an individual are experiencing the world. The result is God. How such a relation is possible, the intellect is not fortunate enough to know. Thus it calls this mystery as "Ignorance or Insentient matter (Maya)". The primitive priciple of appearance, which is essentially one, is called as ignorance or the insentient matter especially when we take into account the predominance of its manifesting and projecting power; and the same is called the veil or ignorance (Avidya) when we take into consideration the predominance of its enveloping power. Thus the objective principle, of which the projecting power is superior to the concealing power, is the limiting condition of God; while the same principle with its enveloping and concealing power is the limiting condition of the individual. The projecting power predominent in God follows from His being the creator of this great world. But he is always conscious of his free-state, and hence is untouched by the concealing power. The individual, on the contrary, labours under the ignorance of his true nature, owing to the predominance of the concealing power and the absence of the projecting power, thus feels incompetent to create the universe as God does. The projecting power is the cosmic power of God.

Therefore all methods of logic fail to estimate and give the true idea of God or world or individual. That does not mean that there is no way to know the reality. The only way to experience the reality is non-sensual integral intuition. This has been discussed briefly in p. no. 26 under the title "What is Integral Intuition".

10

Conclusion

The inadequacy of the philosophic equipment of the Western thinkers in comparison with the Sanatana method does not mean that there is nothing good in them. Kant, Hegel and Whitehead are some of the greatest thinkers the world has produced and their monumental contributions to the fund of knowledge are indeed marvellous. They present different faults of the wisdom of the world and the part they play in chastening the human being in its endeavour to know Truth is not only important but indispensable from the point of view of the student who wants to have clear thinking and logical approach to facts. These thinkers played a significant role in stimulating human understanding in the direction of its ultimate limitations and the realisation of its highest possibilities in its search for Reality.

Kant's researches may be regarded as the strongest foundation of modern critical philosophy and the turning point in the western attitude to the nature of truth. It was Kant who pointed out that—we need not be overconfident of our faculties of knowledge and there are serious defects in their ways of working. He stated that we cannot see Reality with our eyes or any other sense organ, for the senses are involved in the limitations of the space-time constitution. There is no such thing by which one can sense Reality, as we sense the things of the world. To sense Reality, is impossible, for our body structure is in space and time, which have the character of restricting the operations of anything existing or moving within their sphere. Also, we cannot think by mind about Reality, for the mind also works in terms of the categories of quantity, quality, relation and modality, which have many controlling devices that restrain the mind from going beyond their limits. The moment the mind begins to think, it finds itself hemmed in by these categories from all directions and what the mind thinks is thus, what the categories are. Like the frog in the well of the fable, the mind moves within the framework of the categories and thinks that Reality is confined to their structure. Even Mathematics and Physics or any other branch of science cannot lead us to Truth, because they do work on the hypothesis of the empirical reality of space, time and the categories of thought and world. The conclusions of these sciences may be correct as far as the world of these structural limitations are concerned, and we may well follow their lead in our abidance with the laws of the environment in which we all live, for we can never discover that we are wrong as long as we are circumscribed by space, time and the categories which will not allow us to know what is beyond them. But the foolishness on the part of Kant is that he bars us from having any insight into Reality by any means; which is not so, for we have the non-sensual intuition. It is true that with the aid of the reason in us, we cannot have any insight into Reality, for, the reason is also limited to the categories and cannot help out from forming a false conception of Reality in terms of the categories. There is, thus, no metaphysics of Reality in the sense of any right knowledge of it, without non-sensuous intuition, for, we are always within a phenomenal world, and our faculties of knowledge are also involved in it.

The charge of unascertainability of the correspondence between the nature of Reality and our thoughts about it is valid only if we subscribe to the assumption that the mind knows only ideas. The Kantian phenomenalism is the natural corollary of the assumption that I have already pointed out, that, though the contents of knowledge are appearances, it is Reality that we know. So the nature of reality does not transcend our experience and it is Reality, not ideas that are perceived. When the mind apprehends reality, the contents of apprehension are not the object of apprehension, and they become so only for retrospection when again the contents of retrospection are not the contents of primary apprehension. So the objection usually urged against "the correspondence theory" will stand only if we hypostatise the appearance into an object of apprehension.

When therefore it is said that what we think should correspond to the nature of reality, it means that—what we think of the Real in a judgement should conform to what we are led to think of the same in other judgements. Whenever we judge we affirm some predicate of Reality and this affirmation should correspond to the nature of Reality disclosed in other judgments made in reference to the same point in Reality. The correspondence is between the 'what' contained in one judgement and the 'whats' contained in other relevant judgements. It is not a correspondence between the contents of knowledge and something beyond knowledge but between the nature of Reality in other judgements. In other words, when an ordinary man says that what he thinks of a particular thing must correspond to its real nature what he means is that his judgement about it made here and now must agree to other judgements that he may be compelled to make about it hereafter. That judgement which exercises a more constraining element upon him is accepted by him as the nature of Reality and it is the standard by which he judges the truth of another judgement which he makes about the same object but with less constraint.

If from the standpoint of common sense such a conformity between one judgement and another judgement or other judgements is called correspondence between knowledge and Reality, it is because 'for the naive knower-that is, in advance of epistemological criticism—there is no difference between what appears to him and what exists. He treats what appears to be as being the very existent itself; and in so far as his knowledge is veridical is right in doing so'. So, it is contended that because of the subjective conditions that enter the determination of the contents of experience, no knowledge can be regarded as revealing the nature of Reality. Then no knowledge is possible. For knowledge presupposes a subject, and what is an intellectual construction put upon what is given by reality to the subject. A knowledge that is not in relation to any mind is inconceivable. This truth which is so self-evident has been seized by the idealists and interpreted to mean that there is no Reality apart from empirical consciousness.

Thus mathematics, physics (including all other branches of science) and metaphysics are all good as laws of phenomena, but unhelpful for our knowledge of Reality.

Then, what can we know? Kant's answer is: Phenomenal. We cannot know Reality, because we have no means which are outside of phenomena. We are in phenomena and it is futile to imagine that with our intellectual equipment we can have even a glimpse of it. Kant's greatness comes out when he accepts that we would have known Reality if we had been endowed with what he calls an "Intellectual intuition", which, in his system, is knowledge independent of the categories of space, time and thought, but he does not feel that any human being can hope to possess such a faculty, for everyone is within phenomena. This is where and how he fails to recognise the Reality propounded in the Upanishadic texts in which the Sanatana method has been expounded.

This incisive analysis of the Kant is wonderfully equipped to meet the self-complacent attitude which overestimates human powers and makes man live in a world of vanity and ignorance. Further, Kant's great work, **Critique of Pure Reason,** is a masterpiece of acute thinking, logical deduction and honesty of approach in the human world, and it forms a necessary field of training for anyone interested in subtle thinking and comprehensiveness of argument, which is like the Nyāya and Vāiśaiṣika philosophies of the East.

Kant wrote that we have no knowledge of the subject in itself, which as substratum underlies this "I". Even the inner and sensible intuition of our mind and intellect is not the Self proper, as it exists in itself—that is not the transcendented subject—but only an appearance that has been given to the sensibility of this. We should also have to allow the subject an intelligible character, by which it is indeed the cause of those same actions as appearance, but which does not itself stand under any conditions of sensibility, and is not itself appearance. So, I have no knowledge of myself as I am, but merely as I appear to myself. Based on practical reason, a person's true intelligible Self is identical with God and is truly free. In this regard the Sanatana perspective is as follows—As the Transcendented Self we are identical with the Ultimate Reality. Because the Self is our true absolute, essential, unconditioned and perfect Self. The Self, sees everything by its own light, no one sees it. It gives intelligence to the mind and intellect, but no one gives it light. This is the Self, the supreme being, the ancient. It never ceases to experience infinite joy. It is always the same. It is consciousness-existence-bliss itself. It maintains our unbroken awareness of identity. It is the witness, revealer of all things. It is the eternal reality, omnipresent and all pervading. Such a Self can never be grasped by senses, mind, intellect, reason, mental or intellectual intuition, but can be experienced as a supreme existence by non-sensuous super intuition only. As the Western philosophers have taken up only a part of Indian Philosophy and tried to propound in their own way according to the circumstances in which they were dwelling by their mind, intellect and reasoning; they could not experience it. Therefore they lack this ancient true perspective.

So, Kant does deny the existence of God, though he holds that we cannot know him through our senses, mind and reason, for he postulates the existence of God on the basis of the moral urge for perfection surging within us. The affirmation of God, freedom and immortality is a subsequent phase of his thought, on different grounds. His study of the nature of Human duty in society and the development of his thought on aesthetic beauty are important enough to catch the attention of any serious student of philosophy.

Almost all that has been postulated by the different philosophical thinkers and scientists of the West was propounded well thousands of years ago in the East in the Upanishads, Bhagavad Gita and other texts expounded by the different philosophers of the East. There is nothing new that they have added but they all are falling short of what has been shown in the East. Even in the East all schools of philosophy are not perfect in themselves but are only different stages leading us towards the Absolute. The authenticity of our knowledge and the instruments of our knowledge has been very well discussed in the Modern Indian logic propounded by Gangesha Upadhyaya (around 500 AD) within the precincts of the Ancient Indian logic expounded by Rishi Kanada (around 400 BC) which is based on the Upanishads (Date unknown).

Though the western philosophers do not add to the wisdom of Sanatana method (Vedanta), they help for the fortifying of it with a powerful weapon against onslaughts from ill-informed sources. The logic of the West as well as the East would be a good companion to the knowledge of the East. As the aim of philosophy is right living, genuine real philosophy, worth its name, is expected to enable one to live the truest life possible—a life of wisdom, free from the imperfections by which ordinary unphilosophical life is characterised. Philosophy is neither an intellectual diversion nor an academic pedantry overlooking the facts of experiences in the world; neither a feat of empty scholarship nor a mere hobby of the care-free mind; but the intelligent analysis of the immediacy of life as a whole, an examination of the implications of experience, and a scientific theory evolved out from such wise meditations for the purpose of regulating the functions which are responsible for the various phenomena of the individual's consciousness. Philosophy is, therefore, the great art of the perfect life, a life where the common notion of it is transcended, and Supreme Being which is identical with existence-consciousness-bliss itself, is realised.

To realise that Supreme Being we have to accept the value of the different Schools of Philosophy (Both East and West) as stages leading to and representing partial aspects of the philosophy of the non-dual Absolute. We should also have to blend them properly, understand them in a proper perspective and utilise them to gain the non-sensual institution as stated in the Sanatana Method. For that let us try to see how all the philosophies get blended into (Vedanta) the Sanatana Method. It (the Sanatana Method = Vedanta) is *Absolute Realism :* The physical universe is independent of individual minds; it appears material when viewed by the individuals, but is ultimately a mode of the spiritual reality. It is *Idealism:* the universe is an expression of the cosmic mind and the values of life are the expressions of the individual minds. It is *Empiricism:* The individuals receive sensations from the physical universe outside, which is independent of their thinking; God is above man and appears in the form of the universe. It is *Rationalism:* The forms of individual knowledge are constituted of the nature of the individual mind, and even the whole universe is determined by the nature of the necessary and universal laws of the cosmic mind. It is *Voluntarism:* The urges of the will dominate the individual nature and subject it to suffering; the cravings of the will in man restrict the functions of his intellect and make him rationalise the wishes buried in the conscious bottom of his psychological unconsciousness, though the will can be overcome by the higher reason and discrimination. It is *Dualism:* There is, as far as the human life in the world is concerned, a difference between the sensible and the intelligible, matter and mind, individual and God, the actual and the possible, appearance and Reality, and one has to therefore follow the laws of the universal which is above phenomena. Only in and after Self-Realization such distinctions are abolished. It is *Realistic Idealism*: Nothing that is existent can essentially be other than Pure-Consciousness. All existents are subordinate to it. The universe is dependent on the Real. God is the dynamic cause of the universe. It is *Pragmatism:* The true has also a practical value. The world of sense has a practical reality, because it leads to successful action. The existence of God of the universe has to be admitted, and this hypothesis is indispensible to account for life. It is *Indeterminism:* Man's essential nature is spiritual consciousness which is free and is above all determinations in the universe. It is *Determinism:* The relative individual is limited to mind and body which are subject to the operation of universal laws. It is *Evolutionism:* All things are product of development and tend to unfold themselves through several forward and backward movements in their final ascent to the Absolute. It is *Phenomenalism:* The sense universe is a realm of changing appearances or phenomena of the Real, and human knowledge is limited to these phenomenas. It is *Transcendentalism:* The Absolute is above all the categories of the universe, as the universe is an illusion. It is *Immanentism:* God is the indwelling and animating principle of the universe. It is *Agnosticism:* Reality is inaccessible to mere human beings by their thinkers.

Kant's Agnosticism contends that intellectual intuition form no part whatsoever of our faculty of knowledge, it follows that the employment of the categories (of understanding) can never extend further than to the objects of experience. Reason and sense perception cannot prove the existence of a divine supersensible Being or world, which transcend human's empirical experience. This perspective of Kant coincides in one sense with the Sanatana view-point. But actually, there is a divine realm and a personal God too which is a omniscient and omnipotent source from which occurs the birth, continuance and dissolution of this world. This personal God, who dwells in Higher Heavens (Brahma loka), is the First and highest manifestation of the Absolute Self in the finite universe.

Endowed with name and form, he possesses a distinct personality. He is the uncaused first material cause, as well as efficient cause of the orderly universe regulating the cosmos from within, as He is all pervading. This manifestation of God is also not perceivable by reason or sense-perception but is perceivable by a divine vision obtained by his grace only. Thus, there is no doubt that the Ultimate Reality cannot be perceived by senses and reason. So it is Agnostic. At the same time it is transendental as told before. For, an illusion cannot be perceived without a base. The basal conciousness on which this illusory universe is super imposed is the ultimate Reality.

It is *mysticism:* The Absolute is directly realised in spiritual intuition and Being. It is *Pantheism:* The stuff of the universe is not outside God. It is *Theism:* God is the cause of the manifestation of the universe and rules as its Lord. It is *Absolutism:* The absolute is the only reality, and its essence is consciousness. The universe and the individuals are its manifestations or appearances. It is *Mechanistic:* Events follow the laws of space-time in the world of sense-perception and understanding. It is *Teleological:* All motion and activity is directed by God, the final cause, who determines the universe by the law of His Being to which the universe with its contents is originally related.

Thus the Sanatana philosophy (Vedanta) accepts all philosophical theories, but with reservations, as different sides of truth, and not the whole truth. Because all are necessary at different stages for the students who are treading the spiritual path at different phases. So the Sanatana view is a synthesis of all philosophies as well as transcendence of them in a philosophy of the non-dual consciousness which sublimates all existences in its supreme essence. True religion is the practice of this philosophy and this is the religion of the universe, applicable to all human beings, relative to their positions in the scale of the development of their consciousness. Faith, reason and experience, theory and practice, art and religion, service, love and charity, purification, reflection, meditation and realisation, go hand in hand in this philosophy.

The Sanatana Philosophy is a practical, living one, and not simply a theory of the universe, God, individuals, Pure Self, etc...; but the exposition of the nature of one's practical life. It is actually a commentary on life, far from those who think that philosophy is divorced from life and that philosophy is unconnected with the concerns of existence in the world. It is the science which opens up, not only for me but for everyone, the true meaning and value of Human endeavour, the significance of embodied existence in the realm of experience, and enables one to lead a worthy and glorious life here for the purpose of rising to the Blissful Absolute, in which the universe is realised as identical with one's Self, to which nothing other than the Self does ever exist, and as the result of which realization the man becomes the saviour of all things and Beings.

But remember, we need not be too eager to cherish either a fanatical adherence to what is ours or a contempt for what is alien. Knowledge is not the property of any community, race or country and thus has no national barriers. It succeeds when it is honest enough to accept what is of worth and substance, wherever it be found. The East and the West are seeking a common purpose, and it is not true that the 'twain shall never meet', the sense of spiritual values has to rise in all human beings for a universal change.

Everyone knows well that condensation of any thought is likely to take away much of the value of the original. But still I have tried my best to put in a nutshell the views of Kant and Sanatana Philosophy stressing on the limitations and inconsistencies in the thoughts of Kant along with other Western thinkers, trying to correct them by making them to realise their mistakes by presenting the Sanatana philosophy in a simple lucid manner. I expect that the readers will gain a discriminative knowledge of Eastern and Western thought, especially of Sanatana and Kant's philosophy.

Hari Om Tatsat

APPENDIX I

Kant and Shaivism—A Comparative Study

It is very much interesting to note that the Shaivism (The Trika Philosophy of Kashmir, India) had anticipated the German Philosopher Kant a thousand years before in the analysis of experience, as we have already shown before, that in many aspects there are some similarities between Kant and the Samkhya, Nyaya, Vaisheshika Philosophies that had been established long back in the East.

Hume had reduced experience to a passing phantasmogoria of ideas among which there was no binding principle whatsoever. Kant brought about a Copernican revolution in Philosophy in the west by proving that the real experience consists of synthetic judgements which are characterised by necessity and universality. Necessity and universality are not products of experience. They are *a priori* (prior to experience). Senses only provide the data of experience, but understanding imposes its own laws on the data of experience to transform them into synthetic, harmonious, whole of knowledge. Kant called these laws as categories. These are inherent in the very constitution of mind.

But the Trika Philosophy of Kashmir Shaivism maintains that the experience of empirical individual is constituted by ***Māyā*** (a snare which causes bondage) together with her five short breeches/covers ***(Kañcukās)***; namely—***Kalā*** (a small part for limited energy/power), *Vidyā* (spiritual knowledge), ***rāga*** (passion or amorous), ***Kāla*** (time) and *niyati* (restraint).

Kant takes time and space to be forms of intuition. All our experiences are delimited by space and time. Similarly Shaivism also teaches that our experiences are delimited by time and restraints. But remember, space, time and restraints are not the same, they are different things. Thus Kant differs here. Kant believes that man's experience occurs only in a spatio-temporal frame. Similarly Shaivism also believes that man is so constituted by ***māyā*** (ignorance) that his experiences are bound to be circumscribed by ***Kāla*** and *niyati*. The very word ***māyā*** means that power by which experience is measured, i.e., occurred in a particular way *(mīyatai anayā iti māyā)*. In Shaivism the empirical individual is therefore called as ***māyā-Pramātā*** or ***aṇu*** (limited or small). See the difference between space and *niyati*—there are three functions of *niyati*—limitation in space, causality and the measure of a form of things. Liberally speaking we can say that the first two are covered by Kant's categories of space and the category of causality. But strictly speaking a thing which is creating limitation in space cannot be space, it should be different from space, as it is the cause of the limitation in space. So space is not an unlimited substance as Kant thinks. On the other hand, there is nothing in Kant's philosophy similar to the third function of *niyati*. Kant's category of relation can be included in *niyati*. His categories of quantity, quality and modality come under the *kañcuka* *vidyā*, i.e., spiritual knowledge.

Kant's theory is confined only to epistemology. Kant has formulated his theory only with references to knowledge, Whereas Shaivism has formulated its theory both with reference to knowledge and activity. In Shaivism, there are two ***Kañcukās—kalā*** and ***rāga,*** which have no parallel in Kant's system. Both of these are connected with activity. Man is not just a bundle of knowledge, but he is also an active Being. Kalā denotes limitation in respect of action. For, no man is all-powerful like God. *Rāga* denotes his valuation, passions, amorous, craving for things etc. Just as ***kalā*** expresses loss of full sovereignty in the empirical individual, even so ***rāga*** expresses loss of perfection due to its self centredness caused by passions. Such limitations also hinder a person from attaining a super-sensuous intuitive knowledge. It seems that Kant had this problem, due to which he could not reach the Absolute and thus declared agnosticism regarding Pure Absolute Consciousness.

Kant maintained that there are two sources of knowledge—matter and form. Matter is provided by Nature and form is imposed on it by mind. Thus there is dualism in Kant's philosophy. According to Shaivism both matter and form are provided by ***māyā***. Form is provided by *vidyā*, ***kāla*** and *niyati* whereas matter is provided by ***kalā*** and ***rāga*** making the differences: good-bad, mine-not mine, I –not I , etc. As ***māyā*** gives rise to *prakriti* (the first evolved or primordial matter— source of world or root cause of world) by her power of *Kalā*. From this first evolved *prakriti* are derived the intellect; ego and mind. From the ego arise five sense organs, five motor organs and the five subtle elements (which transform into the five gross elements). So both matter and form of knowledge arise from ***māyā***, while ***māyā*** arises from pure consciousness in identity to pure power *(Siva-Sakti)*. Thus there is unmitigated non-dualism in Shaivism.

The most important difference is Kant says that we cannot know the world, self and God by the understanding and the categories. Shaivism also maintains that *māyā* and the phenomena built by her are held by impure and limited means or methods, so the knowledge derived by such means or methods is through distinction making mental constructs and thus we cannot know the real nature of the world, Self and God by perception or reason. But as the knowledge of the world, Self and God is non-distinctive and non-discursive, we can gain their knowledge by non-sensuous intuition. Therefore Kant is Agnostic but not Shaivism.

Kant maintains that the knowledge of the cosmos, Self and God can be obtained only through moral and spiritual discipline. In this regard Shaivism also maintains that the knowledge of the highest reality can be obtained only through spiritual practices which result in developing a non-sensuous intuition. Here Kant again differs, for he accepts only mental and intellectual intuition and never a supersensuous or non-sensuous intuition. With these basal differences Kant is close to Shaivism in certain aspects whereas in some other aspects he is very close to ***saṃkhya, nyāyā*** and *vāiśaiṣika* as shown before. But he is very far away from the Sanatana method (Vedanta), the foundation of which lies in super or non-sensuous integral intuition, which has been very well discussed and proved before.

APPENDIX II

A Critical Analysis of Kant's Lecture on Enlightenment

Kant answered a question on 30th Sept., 1784 in Koṇigsberg, Prussia. The question was—What is Enlightenment?

Answer by Kant (AK)—Enlightenment is man's emergence from his self-imposed immaturity.

Sanatana View (SV)—Enlightenment is man's emergence from illusion by overcoming the ignorance by the experience of Pure Self.

AK—Immaturity is the inability to use one's understanding without guidance from another.

SV—This is impossible, for everyone is being guided since birth and even before birth in the womb too. The truth is without other's (an able spiritual master) guidance nobody can develop the understanding towards englightenment on the spiritual path. So, guidance is needed to a certain extent. How Kant had attained the ability of writing down a critical philosophy without the guidance of his teachers since birth? Did not Kant had any formal education? It is true that bright-students outgrow their teachers but that does not mean that they had no teachers.

AK—This immaturity is self-imposed when its cause lies not in lack of understanding but in lack of resolve and courage to use it without guidance from another. " Have courage to use your own understanding"—That is the motto of enlightenment.

SV—Actually nothing is self-imposed, but, until we are experiencing this external world with empirical reality, every thing is super-imposed on our own Pure Self by the indescribable ignorance. As even it has an empirical reality only and not eternal reality. So, the discriminative knowledge (*vivaika*) and Renunciation *(vaīrāgya)* lead us to enlightenment with the help of a master's guidance. On the other hand, all our wit and courage will only develop our ego resulting in pride and not peace.

AK—Laziness and cowardice are the reasons why so great a proportion of men, long after nature has released them from alien guidance, nonetheless (none-nitity) gladly remain in lifelong immaturity, and why it is so easy for others to establish themselves as their guardians.

SV—This statement is partially true, because laziness and cowardice are obstacles in attaining absolute knowledge through spiritual practices. But it is not right to say that nature has released us, for if nature had released then there is no reason or cause due to which there can be ignorance and its effects—self-imposition (as per Kant) or super-imposition (as per *samkhya* and *Sanatana* method). Nobody is establishing himself as a guardian, but it is due to ignorance of his Pure Self's non-dual nature that one feels insecured and lack of knowledge due to which one accepts another as guardian voluntarily. This is the primordial nature of all species.

AK—It is so easy to be immature. I have a book to serve as my understanding, a pastor to serve as my conscience, a physician to determine my diet for me, and so on, I need not exert myself at all. I need not think, if only I can pay: others will already undertake the irksome work for me.

SV—It seems here that Kant accepts dependence as immaturity. But, a book, a pastor, a physician, etc. . . are all the needs and segments of society; for nobody other than God can have the knowledge of all that is essential in life. So, to make life more effective, efficient, economical, utilitive, and successful; this is not dependence or immaturity, but it is maturity. We have to ask Kant if he wants to build a house, will he not take the help of a mason, etc. . . . will he do everything by himself? For, taking help will be dependence and immaturity. So, it is clear that his definition and understanding about immaturity, which is the base for bondage according to Kant, is itself wrong. Strictly speaking all people are immatured. According to *Yoga Sutrā* and *Sanatana* method—*Ṛtambharā Prajña,* that means actually that person is said to be matured who has got the capacity of holding the experience of the Absolute Truth only. According to this view Kant's theory of maturity and immaturity both are wrong.

AK—The guardians who have so benevolently taken over the supervision of men have carefully seen to it that the far greatest part of them (including the entire fair sex) regard that taking the step to maturity is very dangerous, not to mention difficult. Having first made their domestic live stock dumb, and having carefully made sure that these docile creatures will not take even a single step without a go-cart which they are harnessed to, these guardians then show them the danger that threatens them, should they attempt to walk alone. Now this danger is not actually so great, for after falling a few times they would in the end certainly learn to walk; but an example of this kind makes men timid and usually frightens them out of all further attempts.

SV—This statement is also partially true. Even the Sanatana method states that the human beings are like pet animals of the semi-gods (*Brihadaranyaka Upanishad*). Similarly it is here in this world. But the latter part which states that the Guardians show danger, etc. . . . is not true. Because it is said very clearly that a true master and especially God is more than a million mothers, rescuing the spiritual practitioner from all dangers and lead to liberation, i.e. Enlightenment. The main reason for being bonded to an imperfect master or selfish guardian is that every person due to their passions and afflictions feel insecure and to fulfil their wishes and desires attach themselves to men of similar type. So it has been stated—"People see what they want to see". The truth is that a person who has total renunciation towards all worldly pleasures only can understand this spiritual path by seeing this destructible-temporal-spatial-limited joy and sorrow continuously flowing like a river, so withdraws himself from the worldly activities and meditates, realises and experiences the Absolute Truth.

AK—Thus, it is difficult for any individual man to work himself out of the immaturity that has all but become his nature. He has even become fond of this state and for the time being is actually incapable of using his own understanding, for no one has ever allowed him to attempt it. Rules and formulas, those mechanical aids to the rational use, or rather misuse, of his natural gifts, are the shackles of a permanent maturity.

SV—This statement is also partially true. For in Sanatana philosophy it is accepted that to get birth as a man or woman is very difficult, as the Empirical Self moves from one specy to another specy (there are 84 lakh species) and finally gets a human body. So, while passing through the species of animals, birds, reptiles, insects, trees, plants, etc. . ., the Empirical Self has tendencies or impression of all species imprinted in himself due to which it has a human nature to have food, shelter, sleep, procreation, fear, etc. . ., whether he is fond or not of this state, but he is habituated in such a way that without any external enforcement he is naturally going on. So, either by God's grace or proper guidance by a true master or by own experiences, one realises the truth and gets matured empirically. What is a natural gift? On the physical plane the natural gifts are food, shelter, sexual and sensual enjoyment and attaining worldly pleasures. On the subtle plane he has been gifted mind and intellect by which he got the ability of discursive reasoning, analyzing of his sensual knowledge and imply certain universal and necessary laws by which he binds himself. These natural gifts lead to bondage only and not to liberation. On the supramental plane we have the actual natural gift, i.e., the supersensuous intuition which is not being used even by great intellectuals, like- philosophers (modern), geniuses (scientists) etc. . . . Therefore nobody is restricting anybody in anyway, but it is the ignorance and the animal tendencies that are forcing people at large towards materialism.

AK—Whoever threw them (shackles) off would still make only an uncertain leap over the smallest ditch, since he is unaccustomed to this kind of free movement. Consequently, only a few have succeeded, by cultivating their own minds, in freeing themselves from immaturity and pursuing a secure course.

SV—This is true. Even the Upanishads state very clearly that rarely people do get into rigorous spiritual practices. Here the Sanatana view is—freeing from ignorance and not immaturity. Immaturity is an effect of ignorance, and so is maturity too. As shown before even maturity without discriminative knowledge causes bondage only.

AK—But that the public should enlighten itself is more likely; indeed, if it is only allowed freedom, enlightenment is almost inevitable.

SV—This is totally, not only an absurd statement but also a foolish one too. For this is impossible. Even having given total freedom, nobody will get enlightened. A freedom without true knowledge is very dangerous. It may cause ego-involution; self-destruction; selfish-will, etc., leading oneself to no-where, as he is dragged into worldly affairs by his own instincts which are in indebted or engrained in him, resulting not only in one's own downfall but moreover will be dangerous to society also.

AK--For even among the entrenched guardians of the great masses a few will always think for themselves, few who, after having themselves thrown off the yoke of immaturity, will spread the spirit of a rational appreciation for both their own worth and for each person's calling to think for himself.

SV—This is true. But even here it is to be noted that—it is not "thrown off the yoke of immaturity". Instead it should be—"thrown off the yoke of ignorance", thus getting above the super-imposition by still being in it. This is the best way of working for the good of all.

AK—But it should be particularly noted that if a public that was first placed in this yoke by the guardians is suitably aroused by some of those who are altogether incapable of enlightenment, it may force the guardians themselves to remain under the yoke—so pernicious it is to instill prejudices, for they finally take revenge upon their originators, or on their descendants. Thus a public can only attain enlightenment slowly.

SV—This is partially true. Because no public you can find who has not been placed in the yoke since birth. For every public takes birth and is placed since birth upto childhood in the yoke and under the guardianship of unenlightened parents. So as I have mentioned above, Kant also holds the same—if freedom is given to a public who is incapable of enlightenment, it will be disastrous to all. But again he (Kant) does a mistake by stating—so *pernicious* . . . descendants, because nobody instills prejudices, it is flowing since ages hidden in all. The last part is true—so, let the public undergo a slow enlightenment process according to their own actions.*

AK—Perhaps a revolution can overthrow autocratic despotism and profiteering or power-grabbing oppression, but it can never truly reform a manner of thinking; instead new

* Because prejudices are the input which one inherits formally or informally as part of past learning. There is nothing like final and indibutable cognitive store. Instead cognition is better conceived as something even in process of shifting, rejecting and modifying. When inputs are allowed to stay on without scrutiny they take the form of prejudices.

prejudices, just like the old one they replace, will serve as a leash for the great unthinking mass.

SV—This is not absolutely true. This is applicable only to those who are lustrous, greedy, desirous, ambitious or power hunger. But, there are and were many great men who brought up an intellectual revolution for the good of all establishing true human values which are the eternal (Sanatana) values. Most of the revolutions have brought evolution only and not a devolution.

AK—Nothing is required for this enlightenment, however, except freedom; and the freedom in question is the least harmful for all, namely, the freedom to us to reason publicly in all matters.

SV—This is the biggest mistake done by Kant. For, there is no end to reason, For, it seems to have an end to an individual person, or at a certain time and place only. Actually it follows to an infinite regress. On the other hand, freedom of any type in the empirical state is very dangerous, for it will be finally destructive. The true freedom is to do without any attachment, which is possible only after liberation or is attained by discriminative renunciation only.

AK—But on all sides I hear: "Do not argue" the officer says, "Do not argue, pay" the pastor says, "Do not argue, believe" the priest says; in this we have examples of perversive restrictions on freedom.

SV—These examples show that perverse restrictions on freedom are related to empirical state only, not in the Absolute stand point. For, the officer or pastor or priest are not enlightened or liberated souls. Also, the person who is arguing seems to hinder the natural, smooth, on going daily life and surely will hinder the evolution resulting in obstacles on the path of Liberation.

AK—But which restriction hinders enlightenment and which does not, but instead actually advances it? I reply: The public use of one's reason must always be free, and it alone can bring about enlightenment among mankind; the private use of reason may, however, often be very narrowly restricted, without otherwise hindering the progress of enlightenment. By the public use of one's own reason I understand the use that which anyone as a scholar makes of reason before the entire literate world. I call the private use of reason that which a person may make in a civic post or office that has been entrusted to him.

SV—The reply given by Kant to the question put by himself does not stand scrutiny. For, a reason used privately or publicly as explained by him can only develop intellect and increase ego. Such a person will take for granted for himself to be a leader or Hero or Messiah or Son of God, etc. . . . deceiving the public and himself too. As such a person can never attain eternal peace for himself by such freedom how you can expect him to lead all.

AK—Now, in many affairs conducted in the interests of a community, a certain mechanism is required by means of which some of its members must conduct themselves in an entirely passive manner so that through an artificial unanimity the government may guide them towards public ends, or at least prevent them from destroying such ends.

SV—The role of Government can never be accepted in the path of enlightenment. Not only this but even mass enlightenment has never happened and will never ever happen. Only an individual or a few individuals can have enlightenment. Experiencing enlightenment or total freedom of all is impossible, just like this saying—"No one can fool all people at all times." That means all cannot be fooled, similarly, all cannot be enlightened too.

AK—Here one certainly must not argue, instead one must obey. However, in so far as this part of the machine also regards himself as a member of the community as a whole, or even of the world community, and as a consequence addresses the public in the role of a scholar, in the proper sense of that term, he can most certainly argue, without thereby harming the affairs for which as a passive member he is partly responsible. Thus it would be disastrous if an officer on duty who was given a command by his superior were to question the appropriateness or utility of the order. He must obey. But as a scholar he cannot be justly constrained from making comments about errors in military service, or from placing them before the public for its judgement.

SV—This explanation shows clearly that in different perspectives the person should use reason in different ways and in certain perspectives he should blindly obey and not argue. Such reason is surely empirical and can never be Absolute.

Because a reason, if, it is absolute then surely it should be applicable in all conditions and in all perspectives. Community standpoint, literate world stand point, family standpoint, friends standpoint, etc. . . . all these are empirical standpoints only and not the Absolute standpoint. In the perspective of the Absolute standpoint there is no discrimination, no-division no differences; thus a reason of such sort will be universal and eternal. On the other hand reasons applied in the empirical standpoints always lead to double standardness and double deception.

AK—The citizen cannot refuse to pay the taxes imposed on him; indeed impertinent criticism of such levies, when they should be paid by him, can be punished as a scandal (since it can lead to widespread insubordination). But the same person does not contrary to civic duty when, as a scholar, he publicly expresses his thoughts regarding the impropriety or even injustice of such taxes. Likewise a pastor is bound to instruct his catecumens and congregation in accordance with the symbol of the church he serves, for he was appointed on that condition. But as a scholar, he has complete freedom, indeed even the calling, to impart to the public all of his carefully considered and well-intentioned thoughts concerning mistaken aspects of that symbol, as well as his suggestion for the better arrangements of religious and church matters. Nothing in this can weigh on his conscience.

SV—The basic argument here is itself wrong, for everyone knows that "As many people, so many theories." That means, every man's intelligence level or evolutionary state is different. Therefore the capacity of reasoning thinking, considering and decision making, all differ from person to person. No human being is totally perfect. Thus subordination of the might or religious institutions is unavoidable and inevitable. In such a condition how can anyone get absolute freedom. It is but natural that one seek another for guidance. This is how the society goes on. So, to get out of this jugglery one has to transcend himself and abide by his intuition or God's will to gain absolute freedom, otherwise he will fall a prey to double deception.

AK—What he (the priest) teaches in consequence of his office as a servant of the church he sets out as something with regard to which he has no discretion to teach in accord with his own lights; rather he offers it under the direction and in the name of another. He will say—"Our church teaches this or that, and these are the demonstrations it uses". He thereby extracts his congregation for all practical uses from precepts to which he would not himself subscribe with complete conviction, but whose presentation he can nonetheless undertake, since it is not entirely impossible that truth lies hidden in them, and, in any case, nothing contrary to the very nature of religion is to be found in them. If he believed he could find anything of the latter sort in them, he could not in good conscience serve in his position; he would have to resign. Thus an appointed teacher's use of his reason for the sake of his congregation is merely private, because, however large the congregation is, this use is always domestic, in this regard, as a priest, he is not free and cannot be such because he is acting under instructions from someone else. By contrast, the cleric—as a scholar who speaks through his writings to the public as such, i.e., the world-enjoys in this public use of reason an unrestricted freedom to use his own rational capacities and to speak his own mind. For that the (spiritual) guardians of the people should themselves be immature is an absurdity that would insure the perpetuation of absurdities.

SV—This statement is self-contradictory and immoral too. For Kant says here clearly—servant of church, he would not himself subscribe with complete conviction, good conscience serve. . . . to resign, appointed teacher, etc. . . . on the contrary—he is not free, he is acting under instructions, unrestricted freedom, immature etc. . . . Is this not clear enough showing self-contradiction. It is immoral, because, he is using his own reasons in public against church or religion, i.e., against oath taken by him; which is not only deception towards church but self-deception too, i.e., double deception. On the other hand in the beginning Kant has rejected the necessity of a Guide and here he is propounding—the cleric as a scholar leading the mass through his reason. Why should anybody accept his reason and not depend on their own understanding as mentioned before? Such self-contradictory statements cannot build up any strong position of Kant. Not only this, is not double standardness immoral? So it is true that those spiritual guardians who are imperfect are surely creators of absurdities. For they themselves are imperfect and so, fraud. The Sanatana perspective has alarmed in many ways to be aware of such Masters or spiritual guides who speak something, think something else, do something else, live some other way and so on.

AK—But would a society of pastors, perhaps a church assembly, not be justified in binding itself by oath to a certain unalterable symbol in order to secure a constant guardianship over each of its members and through them over the people, and this for all the time: I say that this is wholly impossible. Such a contract, whose intention is to preclude forever all further enlightenment of the human race, is absolutely null and void, even if it should be ratified by the supreme power, by parliaments and by the most solemn peace treaties.

SV—In the process of human evolution upto a certain stage, bondage and discipline under some religious institution or guide is very much essential, especially until the aspirant has attained a perfect understanding about the Absolute Truth and has tread the right path for it. But one has to be careful before giving up any discipline or bondage; he has to undergo a proper self-analysis and reflection and then take a firm decision. If any institution tries to forcibly stop him or bind him: then it is a crime, for they have stopped the evolution of that person. But expecting some supreme power or parliament or any other social body or peace treaties is foolishness. As even they are not fewer than the former. Because even they are not enlightened, may be corrupt too. In such a condition the aspirant person will have to give up all and surrender to the invisible, all powerful, omnipresent, omniscient God.

AK—One age cannot bind itself, and thus conspire, to place a succeeding one in a condition whereby it would be impossible for the later age to expand its knowledge, to get rid of errors, and generally to increase its enlightenment. That would be a crime against human nature, whose essential destiny lies precisely in such progress, subsequent generations are thus completely justified in dismissing such agreements as unauthorised and criminal.

SV—This statement is related totally to a materialistic world of change, which is illusory and based completely on materialism. Because in the spiritual world this is impossible. For the basic eligibility needed to enter the spiritual world is pure heart (internal organ), simplicity, speaking truth, non-violence (no crime—mental, vocal or physical), etc . . . Thus a perfect moral person is only entitled to go through spiritual practices. Such a person cannot create obstacles or hinder others development. He will never stop others to get rid of their errors. Therefore no age binds anybody and conspires. This universe has an evolving nature. Nobody can ever change the nature of anything, like the hot nature of fire cannot be changed into cold totally by anybody in any time or place. So to think that–somebody can or will obstruct anybody's evolution, is itself totally false.

AK—The criterion of everything that can be agreed upon as a law by a people lies in this question: Can a people impose such a law on itself? Now it might be possible, in anticipation of better state of affairs, to introduce a provisional order for a specific, short time, all the while giving all citizens, specially clergy, in their role as scholars, the freedom to comment publicly, i.e., in writing, on the present institution's shortcomings. The provisional order might last until insight into the nature of these matters had become so widespread and obvious that the combined (if not unanimous) voices of the populace could propose to the crown that it take under its protection those congregations that, in accord with their newly gained insight, had organised themselves under altered religious institution, but without interfering with those wishing to allow matters to remain as before.

SV—This is not possible. For, this is not a permanent solution to the different types of problems faced by the people, and that too in the present world of corruption, especially in the crown level. The only possibility is people should accept self-discipline, self-analysis, self-retrospection and reflection, thereby step by step evade the errors by changing themselves. If this be followed by the populace, the whole society can get enlightened speedily.

AK—However, it is absolutely forbidden that they unite into a religious organisation that nobody may for the duration of a man's life time publicly question, for so doing would deny, render fruitless, and make detrimental to succeeding generations on era in man's progress towards improvement. A man may put off enlightenment with regard to what he ought to know, though only for a short time and for his own persons; but to renounce it for himself, or even more for subsequent generations, is to violate and trample man's divine rights underfoot.

SV—As stated before for all people it is necessary to bind themselves to a religious institution for some time to earn discriminative knowledge, but never bind themselves for a life time. When one feels through the inner being's voice and realises to arise from such bondages, one can give up and enter into the next stage. Thus in the Sanatana threshold, 4 stages are accepted for every man—student life, household life, austrous life and renunciative's life. Depending upon one's own actions of the past births and the present birth a person can go through all by sequence or jump up a stage or two to enter the spiritual world totally. This is the main base of Sanatana view due to which since ages and generations nobody has been stopped from evolving and denied liberation. This will continue for ages and generations to come. Every human being's basic divine right is to attain moral and discriminative knowledge through which he can develop spiritually finally attaining total enlightenment. Thus curbs should be imposed on capitalism, materialism, arms race, exploitation of nature, international-violence, wars, etc. . . . as these are obstacles in an universal enlightenment and peace; such curbs be accepted and followed by all on moral grounds in the good of oneself and the society.

AK—And, what a people may not decree for itself, may still less be imposed on it by a monarch, for his law-giving authority rests on his unificaion of the people's collective will in his own. If he only sees to it that all genuine or purported improvement is consonant with civil order, he can allow his subjects to do what they find necessary to their spiritual well-being which is not his affair.

SV—This is acceptable as the Sanatana perspective also accepts this but under one condition. The control mechanism should be enlightened and non-selfish. For such people (non-selfish elites) only can stop the atrocities of such corrupt monarchs or religious organisations. Without which the authorities will get corrupt and go astray, as seen in almost all religious or political or government organisations and NGO's on the world level. Therefore this formula is also not working efficiently in the present, even though it is good. The root cause of failure is that the elites have themselves become corrupt and deceptive. Thus for the present stage this is not applicable to uphold the society's enlightenment. Thus the Sanatana perspective gives more importance to individual enlightenment and leaves social-enlightenment to the natural process of evolution of the universe.

AK—However, he (the monarch) must prevent anyone from forcibly interfering with another working as best as he can do to determine and promote his own and society's well-being. It distracts him from his own majesty when he interferes in these matters, since the writings in which his subject attempt to clarify their insights lend value to his conception of governance. This holds good whether he acts from his own highest insight whereby he calls upon himself the reapproach, "Caesar non eat supra grammatices". As well as, indeed even more, when he despoils his highest authority by supporting the spiritual despotism of some tyrants in his state over his other subjects.

SV—This is absolutely true. But again, remember what has been told before. The central and ruling mechanisms should work with total cooperation unselfishly. Then only this mechanism will work, whether it is democracial or monarchic or religious. But in this present age this has failed. All have become self-centred, thus selfish and thereby extremists have been moving on a totally corrupt and terrorist path, even misusing religion, power and knowledge for selfish and communal ends without keeping in view the development of the society and the universe as a whole. The Sanatana values are not such and there is no room for such conditions to come up, for it has propounded only human values which lead human being in general towards enlightenment by creating a superb infrastructure of the society, dividing it into four divisions—elites, governance, tradesmen and society servers, who co-ordinating with each other, help each other to live a happy life here morally and attain the goal of life, liberation. Look into the Indian history as written in epics, (but not as altered and put forth by the invaders), so fantastic it was, the whole civilisation was physically, mentally, intellectually and morally enlightened (see Chandogyopanishad). It is the people of polluted and corrupt western society, who just think high and speak about morality, but actually are totally immoral and inhuman are the root cause of all types of chaos in the present world. Really it is astonishing that such people are speaking of human rights who are not even ready to lead a human life, who are trying to divide countries and destroy their peace and culture. May God enlighten them with proper knowledge of themselves and the good of the society. I call the whole world to adopt Sanatana way of life, especially the western society, If they all wish world peace and positive evolution of all.

AK—If, it is now asked, "Do we presently live in an enlightened age?" The answer is "No, but we do live in an age of enlightenment." As matters now stand, a great deal is still lacking in order for men as a whole to be, or even to put themselves into a position to be able without external guidance to apply understanding confidently to religious issues. But do we have clear indications that the way is now being opened for men to proceed freely in this direction and that the obstacles to general enlightenment—to their release from their self-imposed immaturity—are gradually diminishing? In this regard, this age is the age of enlightenment, the Century of Frederick.

SV—This is a mistaken stand by Kant. As, we were and are in an age of scientific-materialistic-physical enlightenment only, not even in a psychic enlightenment, thus no question of spiritual enlightenment. In an age of immorality, pollution (both physical, ecological, mental, intellectual, moral, etc. . . .) and corruption, nobody can dream of an age of enlightenment. Therefore Sanatana's stand is that individudal enlightenment (spiritual) is possible, and all related to such a person can speedily evolve towards liberation. According to the mythological texts which propound Indian history, there had never been an age of total spiritual enlightenment and never will be, but, only a few liberated souls (totally spiritually enlightened) were existing and are existing even now in this world. According to the Vedic texts it seems that in the beginning of the universe, there existed an enlighted age; but later on due to degeneration of the elites the universe faced an age of enlightenment and now due to degeneration in all sections of the society we are going through a totally absurd, immoral and on inhuman age, in which only double deception and intellectual exploitation is going on reducing human being to worse than animals.

AK—A prince who does not find it beneath him to say that he likes it to be his duty to prescribe nothing, but rather to allow men complete freedom in religious matters—who thereby renounces the arrogant title of tolerance—is himself enlightened and deserves to be praised by a grateful present and by posterity as the first, at least where the government is concerned, to release the human race from immaturity and to leave everyone free to use his own reason in all matters of conscience. Under his rule, venerable pastors, in their role as scholars and without prejudice to their official duties, may freely and openly set out for the world's scrutiny their judgements and views, even where these occassionally differ from the accepted symbol. Still greater freedom is afforded to those who are not restricted by any official post. This spirit of freedom is expanding even where it must struggle against the external obstacles of governments that misunderstand their own function. Such governments are illuminated by the example that the existence of freedom need not give cause for the least concern regarding public order and harmony in the commonwealth. If only they refrain from inventing artifices to keep themselves in it, men will gradually raise themselves from barbarism.

SV—Even today everybody dream of such a king or prince or ruler and especially in India it is titled as Rama rajyam—a state without any corruption, pollution and exploitation; But with total freedom, peace and harmony, everybody caring for others, respecting each other, leading to a dignified life with all worldly pleasures and spiritual evolution. Usually every political party, during elections promise to give such a governance which will make the above said dream true. But it has not happened upto this day and will never happen. So no country is left which has moral values and all countries at present have modern materialistic culture in their society. All good morales are in the books and were to a certain extent, may be, in the past sometime.

In the Vedas and other scriptures it has been elaborately discussed about the different levels of freedom and bliss beginning from an Emperor who is young without foes, fully enlightened, attained all worldly pleasures, no pains or afflictions of any type, etc. . . . and that too is actually just a drop from the ocean of Absolute Bliss. To have a society full of such enlightened men is impossible. To think and dream of such a prince, government and elites is utter foolishness in the present condition. Instead of wasting time and energy in trying to attain such an objective, it is better to try for one's own enlightenment, i.e., to establish oneself in Absolute Bliss through discrimination, renunciation and knowledge of Pure Self, thereby toppling the veil of ignorance and ego.

AK—I have focussed on religious matters in setting out my main point concerning enlightenment, i.e., men's emergence from super-imposed immaturity, first, because our rulers have no interest in assuming the role of their subjects, guardians with respect to the arts and sciences, and secondly because that form of immaturity is both the most pernicious and disgraceful of all.

SV—It has already been discussed well that self-imposition of immaturity is not bondage and emergence from the same is not liberation or enlightenment. But, emergence from illusion by overcoming the ignorance by the experience of Pure Self is enlightenment or liberation, while the experience of this external world with empirical reality by the Empirical Self is bondage, and bondage is due to the indescribable ignorance which has super-imposed the trinity of empiricism on the Pure Self. It is not right to blame either the rulers or immaturity of oneself for what is going on. Each and every individual is equally responsible for his own condition and the present state of society. Once we realise this and become self-restraint; then surely a magical spiritual (not only intellectual) revolution with a positive evolution will take place. But it seems even this will be a dream. So, I stress again to begin with oneself, i.e., every individual.

AK—But the manner of thinking of a head of state who favours religious enlightenment goes even further, for he realises that there is no danger to his legislation in allowing his subjects to use reason publicly and to set before the world their thoughts concerning better formulations of his laws, even if this involves frank criticism of legislation currently in effect. We have before us a shining example, with respect to which no monarch surpasses the one whom we honour.

SV—This statement is true but limiting itself to the physical plane. But it seems that those days have gone, when we had kings who loved wisdom and were humble enough to accept criticism and change laws for the good of all. Nowadays our rulers are powermongers, deceptors, corrupts and even criminals. In such a condition, Kant's view which is everyone's wish is just a dream. For this the spiritual power—i.e., intuitional power of the general populace should be uplifted through proper education, religious austerities, discrimination between good and bad, moral and immoral, materialism and spiritualism, consumerism and satisfaction, etc. . . ., so that the society can raise above their temporal selfish ends and think about eternal good and bring down all absurdities in the society and the state. But as far liberation is considered, it has nothing to do with the prevailing conditions of the society and state, instead it depends upon one's own mental conditions and how much he can distract himself from the external absurdities without giving any importance to them and by surrendering to the supreme eternal Being (God) through meditation and other spiritual practices.

AK—But only a ruler who is himself enlightened and has no dread of shadows, yet who likewise has a well-disciplined, numerous army to guarantee public peace, can say what no republic may dare, namely—"Argue as much as you want and about what you want, but obey!" Here as elsewere when things are considered in broad perspective, a strange, unexpected pattern in human affairs reveals itself, one in which almost everything is paradoxical.

SV—This is impossible. See History of India, Russia and other countries. Freedom of reasoning has publicly damaged the culture and divided people into small sects with mutual hatred and disharmony leading to communal riots and finally division of the country itself. Because the ruler will loose control, for the army and governing body are all human beings, and the human beings tendency is to favour that which is favourable to them. So, there will be division of society at all levels. Therefore proper control mechanism is the biggest problem of the society and the state both on the physical and the psychic planes. In such a condition the Sanatana view orders the few elites, who are social-conscious and are leading the path of spirituality should guide the public at the grass-root level for the upliftment of the society, continuing their spiritual practices. Because it is only such people who can, by their spiritual intuitional power and knowledge bring a change in the society and build a self conscious moral society. This is a time taking slow process. But still it will work to a certain extent. Again, I would like to remind that even such an activity is also an obstacle for a person who is very much hungry for his own liberation.

AK—A greater degree of civil freedom seems advantageous to a people's spiritual freedom; yet the former establishes impassable boundaries for the latter. conversely, a lesser degree of civil freedom provides enough room for all fully to expand their abilities. Thus, once nature has removed the hard shell from this kernel for which she has most fondly cared, namely, the inclination to and vocation for free thinking. The kernel gradually reacts on a people's mentality (whereby they become increasingly able to act freely), and it finally even influences the principles of government, which finds it can profit by treating men, who are now no more than machines, in accord with their dignity.

SV—Even this is not true but good for society if it is within limits under proper control as stated before. On the other hand nature is a limited thing and therefore cannot lead anybody to the unlimited. Nature is a bonding agent, thus it cannot give absolute freedom. Nobody can attain the eternal by artificial means or natural means, for all means are within the limitations of time and space, which again are illusory. By an illusory thing how anyone can experience reality and attain absolute freedom and absolute peace to rest in absolute bliss? So, the only way to attain such a bliss is to become introvert and experience the Self, which is the non-dual absolute and pure real existence-consciousness-bliss. For, where there is duality there is sorrow, because duality is due to ignorance, which is a veil over our own Pure Self. So, unveil the ignorance by Pure discriminative self-knowledge and be it.

Hari Om Tatsat

APPENDIX III

We the publishers had circulated the manuscript of this book to many scholars who have a bit of command over both Eastern and Western Philosophies. Most of them have appreciated but a few have raised some objections. In this appendix the author is trying to reply them briefly.

Before answering some objections often raised by learned scholars, I would try to depict some realities which will itself answer most of the objections often raised by learned scholars.

"pratyakshain ānumitya ca yastupayo na budhyatai
Ainam vidanti vedaina tasmat vedasya vedata||"

—Kumarila Bhatt, *Mimansa.*

Dualism or non-dualism of different types is well in the experience (sensual) of all the people, both literate and illiterate. Therefore the purpose of the Vedas is not to propound all that is known by the senses, inference or reasons. But it is meant to propound that which we cannot grasp by the different means of knowledge. So what the Vedas and Upanishads do is that they start with the world as it is and take the aspirant beyond it by negating what we experience by the different means of knowledge. This is called as *"Adhy ārop āpavad ābhy ām Nisprapancam prapancyatai"*. It is Absolute non-dualism which is very hard to understand and experience. Thus all the stories in the Upanishads are trying to make an aspirant to realize the absolute non dual self by negating the illusory world. Therefore the meanings of all statements have to be decided accordingly, which has been done very logically by Acharya Shankara.

It is true that the later Ramanuja, Madhva, etc., have written different commentaries and tried to show that Upanishads do not teach Absolute non-dualism, but they have been very well refuted by the later *Advaitins* in *Brihat Prasth āna Trayi (Citsukhi, khandanakhandakh ādya, Advaita Siddhi, etc.,).* Also, if we see back into the History of Ancient India and especially the Indian Mythology, we shall find that degeneration and devolution is the main reason for the present diversified knowledge of the literate too. As told in the *Gita*—*"Sa kalainaiha mahata yogo nastah parantapa"*. Not only physically, Socially, Economically and politically we have degenerated but also intellectually and spiritually too we have degenerated. Even though the present scientific modern world boost up themselves for the present state of evolution and also the philosophers as Kant himself stated that, "Philosophy up to now (until this time) has not made any progress and had remained involved in fruitless debates". But this is not the truth, it is vice-versa in the East. That may be in the west but not in the east. I too have mentioned in p. no. 50 "Philosophy has really made more remarkable progress than before. My statement is just in comparison to science only. As per the quoted Gita verse we had almost lost the tradition which was revived by Krishna and later on again we lost in the beginning of Kaliyuga which was revived by Acharya Shankara. Now again it is the need of the time that the scholars should over come delusion and illusion, get together giving up all prejudices and the craze of materialism for reviving the Sanatana tradition which has been clouded by some temporal good looking dangling illusory applied sciences and philosophies.

In this book the words 'seer', 'sages' and 'saints' are used for the Ṛiṣis (masters/teachers) who have given us the Vedas. I have not used these words either for Shankaracharya or for saints like Ramanuja, Madhva, Vallabha, etc...

Now let us go through some objections that has been raised by some scholars-

1. Prof. R.S. Bhatnagar of Jaipur, India has pointed out that Kant has not received the attention he deserves as the work is clouded by other western approaches, which also remain unsufficient.

   For this I would like to say that this is a concise work, thus I am not dealing all of his vast works in toto. The major thoughts have been dealt enough as per other scholars too who have read this manuscript and have given their acknowledgements.

   He has said that True philosophy is of my (authors's) personal pereference but True Philosophy is not a matter of personal preference because Truth cannot be a personal property or Truth cannot be many, it is universal, one and one only. To realize that Absolute Truth, everybody is treading the philosophical path. It is clear in the Upanishads, Gita and other Sanatana texts that everyone cannot realize it. Usually Singular number is used in the verses-*"Kascid dhirah"* (Katha Upanishad), *"Kascid Vaitti Mam tattvatah"*, etc... So it is not astonishing that even though True Philosophy is one but still many illusory philosophies have sprouted up due to the intellectual exercise of philosophers. But when a person experiences the truth then all other illusory philosophies vanish, just like all rivers merge into the Ocean. Anyway, their illusory philosophies play an important role in the development of a student who is treading on the spiritual path to experience the Absolute Truth.

2. Prof. Bijayananda has raised objection on the claim of Shankaracharya's Absolute Non-dualism as True Philosophy, for he says that when Ramanuja, Madhva and many others have viewed the same Upanishads, etc. and given different commentaries, then how it is possible to claim Shankara's Advaita as True Philosophy? Similar objection has been raised by Prof. R.S. Bhatnagar, Ms. Leela and others.

The reply is already given above. Again to make it clear... 1. They are like the different steps of a ladder to reach the goal, the Ultimate Truth. As per scriptures only rare people can realize it and not all. Thus for the people who have not yet experienced it, it is for them that God himself incarnates in the form of Ramanuja, etc. and have shown different paths. 2. Even it can be due to Kaliyuga that such people take birth and drive away general public from Reality. Only real aspirants can attain Reality. So these Saints can be called as *Kaliyuga pravartaka* or *Kaliyugaposhaka* $\bar{\bar{A}}ch\bar{a}ry\bar{a}s$. 3. On the other hand in the *Brihat Prasthān Trayi (Cit Sukhi, Advaita Siddhi* and *Khandana Khanda Khādya)* all arguments of other *Acharyas* have been very well refuted. Against *this Brihat-Prasthān Trayi* no scholar of any other system has raised any voice. Only some literate fools with their own prejudices are crying out in vain without any authentic traditional knowledge. Especially nowadays the so called professors (most of them) have no knowledge of Sanskrit too. It is true that *"Vādai vādai jāyatai tattva bodhah"* but even this is said *"Mundai mundai matir bhinnah"*. As told before at every stage of evolution the capacity of intuition also differs and thus knowledge. See *Ānanda Mimāmsa* in *Taittiriyopaniṣad.*

3. Prof. Bijayananda has also raised an objection that the non-dual absolute cannot be identified as God (Isvara).

   But this is not true; Non-dualistic Vedanta has to be understood in three different stages. 1. *Ajāta Vāda,* 2. *Dṛishti Sṛiṣhti Vāda* and 3. *Sṛiṣhti Dṛishti Vāda.* The first is for *uttamādhikhari,* the second for *Madhyamādhikhari* and the last for *Mandādhikari.* So depending on this the Non-dual Absolute, God, *Jiva* and World have been very well established.

   Kant was always in such a socio-political condition that he could not openly speak regarding many things. A true philosopher cannot work under any pressure. If as per Bijayananda's statement "Kant is only concerned with limits and scope of knowledge..., Prof. Sorabjit Mishra states—He (Kant) has no backing of a tradition and Prof. R.S. Bhatnagar says—Kant was more under the then socio-political conditions etc", then it is clear that Kant was not at all a Philosopher in totality.

   The words-True Philosophy, Religious-experience and mysticism has been taken by the objectors in a very wrong sense. Lack of a traditional background seems clear in Bijayananda and other scholars too.

4. Prof. Dayakrisha's objections are the same as of others that Advaita Vedanta cannot be claimed as Sanatana because it is disputed by non Advaitik vedantins and other Indian Philosophies.

   I have already answered this. But it is not right to say advaitins have failed to convince others in the philosophical tradition. Because the question is not of convincing or not convinving, but the question is about the necessity of all these different philosophies. According to me it is necessary, just like *"Sthularundhati nyāya"*. To show a small star first a tree is shown, then a big star just above the top of the tree and then finally the small one. Similarly as all are not evoluted equally and all do not have same power of intelligence, etc., these other philosophies are necessary and it is the need that has brought all these into existence. That does not mean all are true. Thus in the conclusion I have shown how all merge in one just like all rivers into ocean.

5. Prof. Indoo Pandey Khanduri has cautioned about the words intuition and category.

I have tried to clarify this at almost all places, but still, I would request the readers to see the context and decide in which sense it has been used. Knowingly I have used the word "Perpetual Categories" for space and time to correct Kant and show him that they are not meager pure forms of intellectual intuition as stated by him, but are illusory. Indoo says that the object of Kant's philosophy is clearly to describe the complex process of knowledge only. But this is not true. Because Kant speaks of Enlightenment and liberation too. See Appendix 2.

Experience, Intuition and Realization—Indoo states that Sanatana method speaks about Realization only and not experience/intuition. But this is not so, according to Scriputures and Shankara's view it is clear that by non-sensuous intuition only one can have Self realization, that is experience of Self as Absolute existence-consciousness-bliss.

I have never equated *things-in-themselves* with ultimate reality, but I am refuting and trying to correct Kant by *thing-in-itself*. No where Kant speaks of Vyavaharika/Pratibhasika and Paramarthika differences, because this is possible only if one accepts superimposition. Thus you cannot apply this to him. So it is necessary to realize the purpose of propounding the *things-in-themselves* by Kant. Then one can understand the present treatise.

Index

A

Absolute (The), 44, 76, 153
- realisation of, 157
- and God, 162

Absolute Truth, 189
Absolute Existence
- Consciousness Bliss, 95, 162
- sanatana method, 158

Acharaya Sankara and logical reasoning, 36
Actions and Experiments, 152
Aesthetics, 53
Age of enlightenment (living in), 193
Agnosticism, 63, 149
- Kant's, 173, 178

Alexander's view on perception, 168
Anticipation of Kant by Vedic Philosophies, 177
Analytical Method of Philosophical disquisition, 70
Antinomies of speculative cosmology, 25-26
Aristotle view on self, 88
Arthur Eddington
- on Philosophy, 58
- on causality, 138

Axiology, 53

B

Bergson's
- intuitional method, 72
- view on life, 86

Bertrand Russel, 59
Biology and human nature, 33
Bradley on Philosophy, 64, 89
Buddhists on self, 87

C

Caird on self, 117
Causal relation (cause/effect), 135-36, 138
Causality doctrine, 137
Categories of space and time, 100
Categories
- of intuition, 22
- forms, 23
- of substance/causality, 23

Categorical imperative, 27
Chemistry and human nature, 33
Church teachings, 188
Cognitive consciousness, 111
- as per sanatana method, 102

Consciousness
- unity of, 100
- of self, 160

Critical/Transcendental method, 67
Critique of Judgement, 29
Critique of Pure Practical Reason, 18, 26, 170
Criticism of Kant, 168

D

Deep Sleep Experience, 92
Dependence and need, 181
Derivative ignorance, 111
Descartes, 62
- psychological method, 72
- on self, 87
- on finite/infinite being, 160

Dialectical Method of Hegel, 69
Divine presence in human, 164
Doctrine of truth and error, 159
Dreamless Sleep bliss of, 94
Dualism/nondualism, 198

E

Eastern Philosophy, 35
Edwards, D.M., 64
Effort, 151
Ego
- of Kant, 156
- as origin of sense organs, 179

Einstein, 59
Elanvital and consciousness, 86
Empiricism and Rationalism, 65
Empirical objects, 128
Enlightenment Kant/Sanatan views, 180, 184, 195
Epistemology, 52
- criticism, 158
- and Kant, 178

Epistemological analysis of perception by Kant, 99
Error (recognizing), 159
Ethics/Ethical
- Theory, 26, 52
- and human nature, 34

Evolution, 189, 191
External Perception, 114
Experience, 85
- world of Kant, 19, 119
- factors, 20
- levels of, 22

F

Form origin of, 178
Freedom of the soul, 152-53, 197
Freedom, 185
- principle of, 153-54
- spirit/level of, 194
- of reasoning–impact of, 196

Free will and necessity, 150

G

Geometrical method of rationalism, 67
God's/God
- consciousness, 116
- existence arguments on, 161, 171
- nature of, 162
- idea of, 166

H

Head of state favouring religious enlightenment, 195
Hegel's dialectical method, 69

Hume's
- scepticism, 66
- on self, 83

Human evolution, 189
Hypothetical Imperative, 27

I

'I' consciousness, 89
Ideas of reason, 24-25
Immanual Kant on self, 88
Immaturity, 181-82
and dependence, 181
Indian/Western history (values), 192
Integral Intuition, 42, 44, 155, 179
Intellectual
- intuition, 170
- revolution, 185

Intellect, Intelligence, 47
Internal Perception, 116
Intuition, 45
- and intellect, 47

Intuitional method Bergson's 72

J

James Jeans
- on significance of space/time, 129
- on casual law, 138

Joad, C.E.M., on cause/effect relation, 138, 154
Johanne, Fichte, 146

K

Kant
- what he says, 18
- outlook, 141
- method, 142
- theory, 178

Knowledge
- origin of, 21
- of the cosmos, 179
- /experience/comparison, 103
- validity/invalidity of, 109
- categories, 70
- of object/self, 112
- nature of, 20, 118
- of space, 131
- sources, 178
- as per Sankhya, 102

Knower/Known/Knowledge, 132

L

Laws of association, 89
Laziness and cowardice, 181
Leibnitz on self, 82
Liberation (Moksha), 77
Life
- philosophy, 55
- principle-Bergson's, 86

Limits of Knowledges, 128

M

Mathematics and human nature, 32
Maths/Physics and reality, 168-69
Mathematical method of rationalism, 66
Materialism, 183
Matter and form–origin of Shaivism, 178
Max Planck, 59

Maya, 128, 165, 177, 179
Metaphysics of Ethics, 18
Metaphysics of Morality, 26
Metaphysical Knowledge, 149
Metaphysics, 51
Method of Philosophy, 61, 72
Milikan, R.A., 59
Mind and material Kant on, 157
Moksha (liberation), 77
Monarch functioning of, 191-92
Mysticism, 53

N

Nature–secrets of, 45
Non-sensuous Integral intuition, 44

O

Objective consciousness, 112
Objections by scholars, 199-202

P

Paralogisms of speculative or Rational Psychology, 25
Passage of Time, 124
Paton, H.J., views, 160
Perceptions
- concept, 97
- empiricists views, 143

Perceiving
- nature of, 105
- as per Realists, 107

Percepts and concepts, 144
Physical Theory of Relations on Space/Time, 129
Philosophy
- purpose, 32, 38
- and science, 31
- need of, 34, 37
- as experience, 49
- classification, 51
- definition, 55-56
- method, 72

Physical world, 147
Physics and human nature, 33
Plato, 58
Postulates of
- morality, 28
- immoratility, 28
- freedom, 28
- existence of God, 29

Pragmatic method, 72
Pragmatic Theory of Truth, 118
Priests-teachings by, 187
Psychology and human nature, 33, 52
Psychological
- method, 70
- of Descartes, 72

Psychoanalysis on consciousness, 84

R

Reality of space, 133
Real self of Sanatana Method, 156
Reality and reason, 69, 167-68
Realists perceptions difficulties/remedy of, 108
Reason, 68
- use of, 185
- freedom of, 196
- commands given by, 18
- ideas of, 24, 158
- study of, 68
- view on, 157

Religious
- discipline importance of, 189-91
- enlightenment views on, 195

Researches of Kant, 167

S

Sanatana
- doctrine of causality, 137
- method, 36, 62, 75, 97, 110
- true philosophy, 89
- philosophy constituents and Vedanta, 172-74

Sanatana/Modern Medical Science comparison, 110
Sankhya/Sanatana method comparison, 104
Sankhya Theory of perception, 99
Sankhian Philosophy, 162
Sankhya realism, 104
Scepticism and Agnosticism, 57
Science and Philosophy, 57
Self, 160
- nature of, 81-90, 93
- identity, 100
- consciousness, 83
- conception of, 117

Sensation, 20
- Kant on, 143

Senses
- intuition of, 22

Sense
- (knowledge of), 97, 170
- experience, 141, 148

Self, Space, Time, 160, 177
Shaivism, 177
on matter and force, 178
Sociology and human nature, 34
Socrates, 58
Socratic Analytical method, 70-71
Space/time/matter
- (existence of), 123
- significance, 130
- knowledge of, 131

Speculative Psychology/Cosmology, 25
Spiritual laws, 156
Syadavada theory of Jainism, 149
Supreme Being (realisation of), 172
Superconscious intuition of God, 164
Synthetic Dialectic Method, 71

T

Taylor, Prof
- on self, 81
- on space/time, 133

Theories of knowledge, 61
Theory of creation of world by God, 165
Things in themselves, 145, 148-49, 155, 160
Time/space concept, 125, 134
Time process, 125
Transcendental
- Background concept of, 102
- idealism, 113
- psychology, 159
- illusion, 113

Transcendence of space in self, 133
Trika philosophy of Kashmir Shaivism, 117

True Philosophy, 41, 72, 77
True Knowledge nature of, 118
True self Nature of, 90
Truth pragmatic theory of, 118

U

Unconditional consciousness, 158
Unity consciousness, 113
Universal Philosophy, 36
Universe concept, 123
Universal event-concept, 131

V

Vedanta teachings, 79

W

Waking/dream states ego, 94
Western Philosophy, 35
Western/Sanatana Philosophy, 167, 171
Western/Eastern Philosophy, 171
What Kant Philosophy says, 17
Why has God Created World, 163
Whitehead on
- self, 87
- causality, 139

William James
- on philosophy, 56
- pragmatic method, 72
- on experience, 85
- on consciousness, 108

World creation of, 163

Y

Yoga Vasistha, 126
- on relativities of space/time, 127